BIBLE STORIES
FOR CHILDREN

Introductions by Ted Harrison

WHSMITH
EXCLUSIVE
· BOOKS ·

CONTENTS

THE OLD TESTAMENT

THE NEW TESTAMENT

Moses in the Bulrushes, page 48

THE OLD TESTAMENT

The Bible is not so much a book as a library of books. Even by people who have no religious faith, the Bible is generally acknowledged to be a collection of some of the greatest writings of all time. For believers, however, the Bible is more than just a great book; it is a holy book, indeed it is the inspired word of God.

The books of the Bible are of many different kinds. Some contain history, some consist of poetry and others are collections of letters. In the Bible the reader can also find myth, parable and prophecy.

For thousands of years the best-known stories in the Bible have been common knowledge to millions of people living in many different lands, times and cultures. The Jews of Jesus' day would have told the story of Noah and his ark to their children. Peasants of medieval Europe would have known the same story from looking at stained-glass windows and colourful wall paintings in their churches. Today children still play with toys of Noah, his family and his animals and there is even a modern opera celebrating the flood. The story of Joseph and his coat of many colours has not only been famous throughout history but has been turned into a rock musical which dozens of schools perform every year.

Indeed people who never even go to church or read the Bible still draw on the images of the Bible to give colour to their language; strong men are frequently likened to Samson and underdogs who triumph against the odds are seen as modern day Davids battling with modern day Goliaths.

The Bible is made up of 66 books and is divided into two sections. The first part, the longest, with 39 books is called the Old Testament. It tells the story of the creation of the world and of the first people, and follows the trials and tribulations of the early Jewish people. Many of the Old Testament stories are important to followers of the three great world religions which worship the one God: Christians, Jews and Muslims.

The Bible stories retold in this book come to us from thousands of years ago. To begin with many of the stories were handed on from one generation to the next by word of mouth and were not written down for centuries. But that does not mean there is anything remote about the stories. The characters of such people as Abraham, Moses and David are described so vividly, they might be living today, we feel we know them so well.

What gives the stories added interest is that the action frequently happens in places we still hear about today, such as Jerusalem and Egypt. Even if we have never been to these places we will know what they are like from television pictures and photographs, and many parts have changed little over the centuries.

While the New Testament, the second section of the Bible, provides the Christian with a special inspiration, the Old Testament has been included in the Christian scriptures for a number of reasons.

Firstly, Jesus was himself a Jew and to understand many of the things he said and did it is important to know about his background. There are many references made by the writers of the New Testament to the Old Testament particularly to point out how prophecies from ancient times were fulfilled in Jesus.

Secondly, the Old Testament provides for Christians many valuable insights into the nature of God and through its poetry provides many of the different images of God.

Thirdly, the stories confirm for Christians their belief that God remains true to all who trust in him.

Families with a religious faith will certainly love reading these stories together. But even families without a tradition of belief will enjoy them.

They are great stories which never grow stale with retelling. They have all been known by and told to children for thousands of years and are part of the common inheritance of all people.

TED HARRISON

THE CREATION

In far distant days the Hebrew people of the Bible were a wandering tribe earning a meagre living by moving from place to place with their herds in search of new grazing land. In the evening they would sit under the vast vault of the star-studded sky and chat and relate familiar stories that had been passed on by word of mouth. Some of these stories gave answers to age-old questions about who made the world, and about the nature of Mankind. In all these stories the early Hebrew people believed the Spirit of God guided them to the answers and to the truths by which to know him.

One of the stories tells how the world began. It is not a first-hand historical account, because no one was there. There are no scientific details, no dates or times. It is a true account nonetheless, for God's Spirit had enabled his people to understand his world and how it came into being. It tells us that the universe has a creator. He has a purpose in his work and his plans are still being worked out. This all-powerful yet loving creator knows each one of us.

This is how the story has come down to us.

In the beginning, when God created the universe, the Earth was empty and uninhabitable. The heaving ocean that covered everything was wrapped in total darkness. And a mighty wind swept over the waters.

Then God spoke and his Word created.

"Let there be light," he commanded, and the world was bathed in brilliance. He separated the light from the darkness. The light became day and the darkness became night. *Evening and morning had come – the first day.*

At God's command the sky was made. It spread like a huge dome above the empty Earth, giving the world air to breathe. *Evening passed and morning came – a second day.*

At God's command dry land rose up from the great waters. The land he called earth and the water, sea. At God's command life came to the earth. Plants of all kinds sprang up. Their roots went deep into the soil and they produced flowers and fruit. *Evening passed and morning came – a third day.*

God set the Earth among the brilliant stars. He caused the Sun to shine on the Earth, making the day. The cool, clear Moon lit the night. The movements of Sun, Moon and stars measured days and seasons for the Earth. *Evening passed and morning came – a fourth day.*

Now God commanded, "Let the waters be filled with life and let birds fly in the sky." The seas teemed with all kinds of creatures and the sky was filled with birds. He blessed his creatures and commanded them to increase in number until they filled the Earth. *Evening passed and morning came – a fifth day.*

Then God commanded. "Let the Earth produce all kinds of animal life, domestic and wild, large and small." So animals began to roam over the Earth – from huge beasts to tiny insects.

Now the world was ready for God's final great act of creation. "They will be like me and they will be able to know me," he said. "They will have power over the fish, the birds and all the animals."

Out of the newly formed earth, God made Man. He breathed life into him so that he would be like his creator. God called the man Adam and gave him the task of naming all the birds and animals.

Then God said, "It is not good that man should be alone. I will make a companion for him." Taking a bone out of the man's side, God created Woman. He called her Eve, meaning Life. He said: "Have many children so that your descendants fill the Earth. You are the masters over my world – all the fish, birds and animals. I have given you grain and fruit to eat and grasses and leaves for the animals." *Evening passed and morning came – a sixth day.*

On the seventh day the Lord God rested. He blessed the seventh day and it was called holy, a day set apart for God. *Evening passed and morning came – a seventh day.*

GENESIS 1 TO 2:1–3, 7, 20–22

Adam and Eve

God made Adam and Eve a beautiful garden to live in called Eden. In the centre stood two magnificent trees: the Tree of Life and the Tree of the Knowledge of Good and Evil.

God told Adam and Eve they could eat fruit from any of the trees – but not from the Tree of the Knowledge of Good and Evil.

Adam and Eve spent many happy hours wandering through the garden. They were naked, but they were not ashamed.

But the snake, the craftiest of God's creatures, began to tempt Eve.

He coiled himself in the branches of the Tree of the Knowledge of Good and Evil.

"Eve," he called softly, "Did God really tell you not to eat any of these delicious fruits?"

"We can eat fruit from any of the trees in the garden," she said, "except for this one. God said that if we even touch it, we will die."

"You won't die," hissed the snake. "If you eat the fruit you will be like God. You will know what he knows. That is what it means to have the knowledge of good and evil."

Eve began to feel less sure of herself. What if the snake were right? Wouldn't it be wonderful to know everything? Slowly, she stretched out her hand, picked one of the beautiful fruits and ate it. She then offered the fruit to Adam. He, too, knew that he should have refused, but he did not. He ate some of the fruit.

Suddenly, they both felt guilty and ashamed. Their eyes were opened to see that life was no longer simple and innocent. They were ashamed of being naked and tried to cover themselves with leaves.

That evening they heard God walking in the garden. They hid in the trees. God called out to Adam, "Where are you?"

"I heard you," replied Adam, "but I was afraid, so I hid. Eve gave me the fruit and I ate it."

Then God turned to Eve, "Why?" he asked. "The snake tempted me," she said.

There was a faint rustling among the leaves. God turned on the snake. "You will be punished for this," he said. "You will crawl on your belly in the dust as long as you live."

To Eve he said, "You will suffer pain in giving birth."

To Adam he said, "You must work hard for a living and one day you will both die. Dust you are and to dust you will return."

So God turned them out of the Garden of Eden. He set the Cherubim, the angelic guards, to bar the way back.

GENESIS 2:8–17; 3

The man gave names to all cattle, to the birds of the air, and to every wild animal;
Genesis 2:20

CAIN AND ABEL

Adam and Eve had many children after they were sent out from the Garden of Eden. Two of their sons were called Cain and Abel. Cain grew up to become a farmer, and Abel became a shepherd.

At harvest time the brothers brought presents to God. Cain brought God some crops, but Abel brought him the best lambs from his flock. God was pleased with Abel's gift but Cain's did not please him. Cain grew angry and scowled.

"Why are you angry?" God asked. "If you work hard you will be rewarded. If not, you may become sinful, and sin will destroy you."

But Cain was jealous of Abel and did not listen to God's warning. One day, while they were working in the fields, Cain attacked Abel and killed him.

God then asked Cain, "Where is your brother, Abel?"

"I don't know," answered Cain. "Am I my brother's keeper?"

"What have you done?" said God. "Your brother's blood cries out to me from the soil. From now on the soil will produce no more crops for you. You must leave your land and wander the Earth as an outlaw."

Cain was horrified. "I cannot bear this punishment," he pleaded. "You are driving me away from

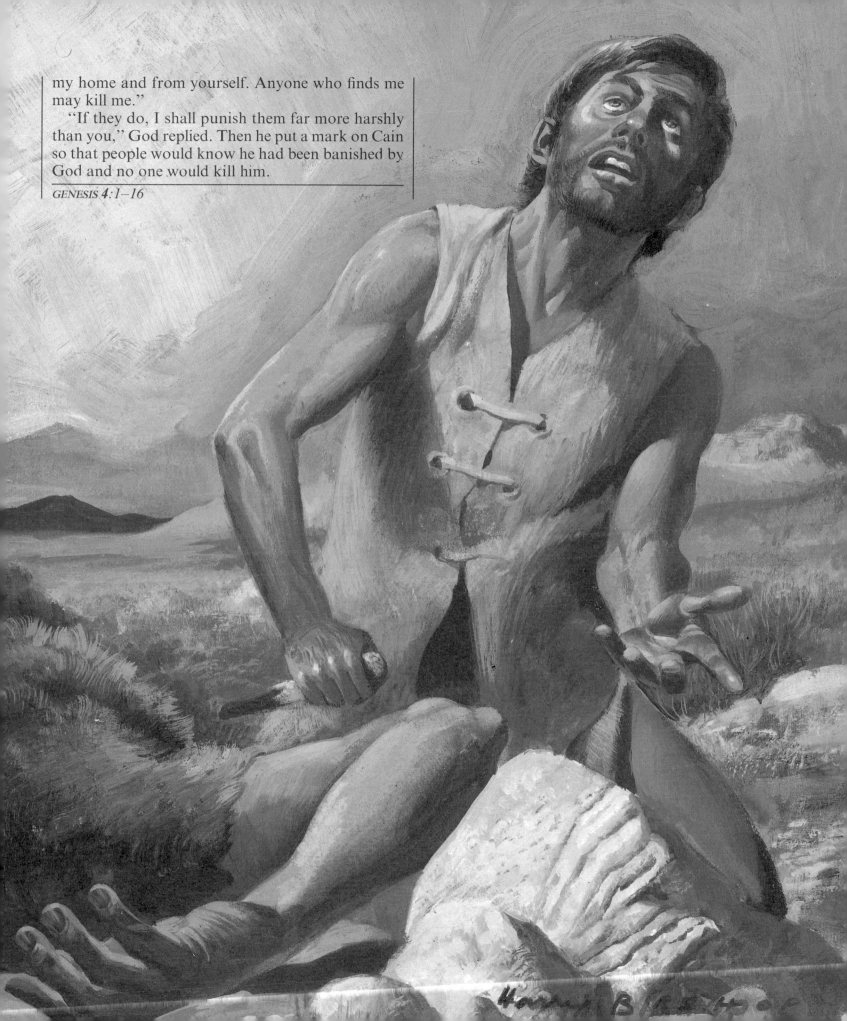

my home and from yourself. Anyone who finds me may kill me."

"If they do, I shall punish them far more harshly than you," God replied. Then he put a mark on Cain so that people would know he had been banished by God and no one would kill him.

GENESIS 4:1–16

Noah and the Flood

The story of Noah tells of a time long, long ago when people had become cruel and wicked.

God looked down on the world which he had made. He was deeply hurt. He felt sorry that he had ever created the human race. "I will rid Earth's face of all people, animals and birds," he said.

But there was one person who truly worshipped God. His name was Noah. He was an honest man who tried to live his life as God wanted. Because of this, God decided to spare him and his family.

God spoke to Noah. "I have decided to put a stop to the evil in the world." He told Noah he would send a great flood that would wipe out all his people – except for Noah and his family.

"Noah," said God, "build a boat for yourself out of good timber. It should have three decks, divided into rooms, and a door at the side. Make it watertight with pitch."

God gave Noah the exact measurements for the boat, or ark as it was called. It would be like an enormous floating container.

"Collect a male and female of every kind of animal and bird there is," God went on, "and take them into the boat with you. Then, when the flood is over they will be able to re-populate the earth with animal life." God also reminded Noah to take on board huge supplies of food.

Noah obeyed God. He and his sons, Ham, Shem, and Japheth, set to work. How the people stared and laughed as they saw them building the great boat on dry land, miles away from the nearest sea. But Noah kept on building. He cut the wood, dragged it into place, pegged the great beams together, and painted on the last of the pitch.

At last the magnificent boat was finished. God told Noah to collect the animals. In they went, two by two – elephants, lions, deer, rabbits, foxes, lizards, monkeys, eagles, everything. Then Noah and his family went into the boat.

Soon, just as God had warned, dark clouds began to gather overhead, until the sky was black. Suddenly the sky seemed to break and torrential rain poured down like a waterfall. At the same time, underground streams burst to the surface and flooded the land.

Slowly the water rose, drowning trees and fields, flooding the cities, and rising until it covered the hilltops. Every living thing perished, but those inside the ark were safe and warm.

After forty terrible days there was a calm outside the boat. The storms seemed spent and no more rain fell. The water began to go down. But it was to be several months before the mountain peaks began to break through the surface of the grey water.

More time passed. Noah now decided to send out a raven to see if it could find dry land. It did not come back. Later he sent out a dove but it could not find the dry, sheltered place it needed and returned to the boat. After seven days Noah tried again. Off flew the dove over the waters. That evening it returned. In its beak it carried a fresh green olive leaf. "The waters are going down and the trees are appearing again," Noah cried joyfully. A week later he set the dove free again. This time it did not come back.

The water had gone and the ark came to rest on a peak of Mount Ararat. Noah and his family finally stepped out on dry land followed by all the creatures. The world was empty, waiting for a new start.

Then Noah built an altar to God and in thanksgiving offered sacrifices of birds and animals. God was pleased with Noah's thanks and made a solemn promise. "Never again will I flood the world to destroy all the people I have made. As long as the world exists, there will be a time for planting and a time for harvesting, cold and heat, summer and winter, day and night." Then God said, "Look up and see the rainbow in the sky. That is the sign of my pact." Noah looked up and there, stretched across the sky, was a beautiful rainbow.

GENESIS 6:5–22 TO 9:1–17

"You are to bring living creatures of every kind into the ark to keep them alive with you, two of each kind, a male and a female;"
Genesis 6:19

THE TOWER OF BABEL

After the great flood the centuries passed and the population of the world increased. Everyone in the world, it was believed, spoke the same language and understood one another.

At some time during those centuries a great migration of people took place. They settled in the Babylonian plain. There, a great civilization grew up. Things were going well for them. There was plenty to eat and everyone lived comfortable lives. But the people began to forget God, they became arrogant and proud.

"With our new discovery," said one man, rising to his feet, "we'll build the biggest city the world has ever known. In the centre we can build a tower that will reach right up to heaven! It will stand so high that everyone will be able to see it for miles around. Then they will know what we are capable of!" There was a chorus of agreement among the Babylonian people.

The great discovery they had made was how to make bricks. They could bake them so hard that they were able to make huge buildings that would last for years. Now they were talking about building a fantastic tower to show off their skill. Not once did they think to thank God for giving them the skill or the raw materials or the prosperity that made the whole thing possible.

The planning continued. "We'll use the new bricks, hold them together with tar and build the tower so that it reaches right up to the sky," said one. "Yes, a tower like that will act as a landmark and keep us all together."

If they had really thought about it, they would have had to admit they meant to show that they were totally independent of God. They had begun to believe that they could do anything. It was a short step from declaring that they were God themselves.

God was angry. This was just the beginning of a major rebellion. Violence and lawlessness would follow, with everyone doing just what they wanted, and soon the world would be as bad as it had been before the flood.

Work on the great tower, the centrepiece of the city, began. Slowly it became higher and higher. They were still building the upper levels of the great monument to man's achievement when God said, "Enough!"

Then suddenly, throughout the great city something amazing happened. People were not speaking the same language any more. One man would try to say something to his neighbour only to be met with blank astonishment. When the man replied, it sounded like babble. God had divided their language. People could no longer communicate with one another. No one could understand what the foreman wanted and the foreman could not understand what his workers were saying. The building of the tower had to be abandoned.

Slowly groups formed who discovered they had the same language. People kept with those they could talk to. They no longer all worked together. Overnight the idea of building a city where they could all live, seemed ridiculous.

At a stroke God had shown that, clever as the people of Babel were, there was only one God, only one Lord of all the universe. The story was also trying to give an explanation of how the different languages of the world began: from Babel groups of people speaking the same language drifted away from one another and settled in new regions to form new nations.

GENESIS 11:1–9

"Let us build ourselves a city and a tower with its top in the heavens and make a name for ourselves,"
Genesis 11:4

God's Promise to Abram

With the story of Abraham and those that follow we begin the history of God's Chosen People, the Israelites, of whom Abraham – at first called Abram – was the founding father. The stories were told by people who lived then. They were handed down by word of mouth and later written down in chronicles.

In the splendid city of Ur, in Mesopotamia, with its fine buildings, there lived a wealthy man called Terah who had three sons. One son, Abram, was married to a beautiful woman named Sarai, but she had no children. Late in his life Terah left Ur taking with him his family and their possessions and travelled northwards to a place called Harran.

When Terah died, Abram had a strange experience. It seemed to him that God was speaking to him. "Leave here and go to a land I will show you. I am going to give you many descendants and they will become a great nation. You will do well in that land and your name will become famous. Through you I am going to bless all nations."

Such instructions and promises could not be ignored. So Abram set off south-westwards to Canaan, the land God had set aside for him. He took his wife and nephew Lot, together with all his possessions. When he arrived in the region, he built an altar and there God appeared to him again. "This is the country I am going to give your family," he said to Abram.

Some time later Abram had a vision. He heard God saying to him, "Do not be afraid Abram. I will shield you from danger and give you a great reward." When he heard this, Abram poured out his great worry to the Lord. Sarai, his wife, did not seem to be able to have children. "I have no son. One of my slaves' sons must be my heir."

Gently, God took Abram outside the tent and said, "Look at the sky

and try to count the stars; you will have as
many descendants as that." Abram
trusted God. He knew in his heart
that God's plan would be fulfilled.
This pleased the Lord, and from
that time on Abram's great faith
in God made him a just man, accepted
by God as a friend.

*GENESIS **11**:31–32; **12**:1–7; **15**:1–6*

Abram's Two Sons

Abram and Sarai had no children. It was becoming difficult to understand how Abram was going to be the father of a great nation. Finally, Sarai decided they must do what many other people did in those days. She had an Egyptian maid called Hagar. Abram was to take Hagar as a second wife so that she could have a child by him.

Abram agreed to this. But when Hagar knew she was going to have a baby, she became contemptuous of the childless Sarai and sneered at her mistress, which upset Sarai greatly.

Abram, fearing more trouble, let his wife take control of the slave. But Sarai took advantage of her position of power and treated Hagar badly. Before long things got so bad that Hagar could bear it no longer. She fled southwards to the desert.

While Hagar was resting by a spring in an oasis, an angel appeared to her. "Where have you come from and where are you going?" the angel asked. "I'm running away from my mistress," Hagar replied.

"Go back to Sarai your mistress, Hagar," the angel told her. "You will have a son and through him I will give you more descendants than anyone can count. God has heard your cries of distress, and you will call you baby son Ishmael which means 'God hears'." Hagar returned to the camp and sure enough, when her time came, she gave birth to a baby boy.

Abram was proud of his son. Ishmael was a lively boy and Abram was beginning to think that the lad would become his sole heir, and eventually take over the leadership of the tribe. After all, Abram was already very old and his wife was well past normal child-bearing age.

Then the Lord God appeared to him. "Abram," he said, "I am going to make this solemn promise to you. You will be the ancestor of many nations. Because of this I am going to alter your name. From now on you will be called Abraham (which means father of many nations). I will be your God and the God of your children. This land in which you are

now a foreigner will belong to your descendants for ever and I will be their God. Your wife also shall have a new name – Sarah. I will make her life overflow with joy because she is going to have a son."

Everything happened as God foretold, and Sarah and Abraham, as they were now called, became the proud parents of a baby boy called Isaac.

Sarah still harboured bad feelings towards her servant and did not like the idea of the two children growing up together. More than that, she hated the idea that young Ishmael would inherit some of Abraham's wealth. She spoke to Abraham. "Send the slave girl and her son away. I don't want Ishmael to get any of your money. It must all go to Isaac." Abraham was very unhappy. Ishmael was also his son and he loved him.

But God comforted Abraham. "Do not worry about Ishmael and Hagar. Do whatever Sarah says, because it is Isaac who will carry on your line. I also plan to give many children to the servant girl's son. His descendants will become a nation too."

So Abraham sent the distressed Hagar and her son off into the desert with food and water. They wandered aimlessly around in the blistering heat until their water gave out. They could not survive for long. Soon Ishmael collapsed and Hagar laid him down under a bush out of the sun. She moved away where she could not see him, "I cannot watch the child die," she cried.

Suddenly a voice spoke to her. "Don't worry Hagar," it said, "God has heard your boy crying. Go and get him and comfort him. He is going to live because God has said 'I will make a great nation from Ishmael'."

As God's messenger finished speaking, Hagar saw that there was a well nearby. Their lives were saved. She put some water in her leather bottle and gave it to Ishmael, who soon recovered.

Although Hagar and Ishmael survived, they never returned to Abraham and Sarah. They travelled as far as the Desert of Paran where Ishmael grew up. He became a skilful hunter. As time passed he married an Egyptian girl and started a family. In time his family became a powerful tribe – the Ishmaelites.

GENESIS 16:1–16; 17:1–22; 21:1–21

Sodom and Gomorrah

Abraham's nephew Lot lived in the city of Sodom. The people of Sodom and the nearby city of Gomorrah led wicked and corrupt lives. God told Abraham that he meant to destroy both cities.

Abraham immediately thought of Lot. "Are you really going to destroy the innocent people as well as the guilty?" Abraham asked. In pity God heard Abraham's cry. Before destroying the cities he sent two of his angels, disguised as men, to see if any good people still lived there. He agreed to spare everyone even if there were only ten people worth saving.

Lot was sitting at the city gate when the messengers from God arrived. He sensed that there was something special about them and he asked them to stay at his house. They agreed and Lot's servants prepared a splendid meal for them.

But word soon went around that there were strangers in the city. The people of Sodom thought that this was a chance to enjoy some violent and wicked sport. A mob gathered outside Lot's house and battered on the door demanding that the strangers be brought out.

Lot tried to protect his guests; he stepped outside, but the crowd surged forward. Lot's guests quickly pulled Lot inside. Then, using powers given them by God, they struck the mob blind.

The messengers told Lot to take his family and leave the city quickly. "But whatever you do, don't look back," they warned.

The sun was rising when Lot and his family reached the little town of Zoar. Suddenly there was a thunderous roar as the ground around Sodom and Gomorrah opened up in a terrible gaping earthquake. Burning sulphur rained down from the sky, consuming everything in its path.

Lot's wife, ignoring the angels' warning, looked back to see the valley in flames. That was the last she ever saw. She died where she stood, turned, it is said, into a pillar of rock salt.

GENESIS 18:20–33 TO 19:1–29

THE SACRIFICE OF ISAAC

One time Abraham's faith was seriously put to the test. Abraham heard the voice of God saying, "Abraham, I know you love Isaac very much, but I want you to take him with you to the mountains of Moriah and to sacrifice him in my honour."

Abraham was devastated. It seemed that God had given him something, only to take it away again. But he was also convinced that whatever God did or said had a good reason behind it. So he loaded his donkey, called two of his men to go with them, told Isaac to get ready and set off.

On the third day of the journey thay came in sight of a high mountain, a fitting place for a sacrifice. "Stay here with the donkey," he said to his servant. Abraham and Isaac collected together the wood they had brought for the sacrifice, the smouldering wood to start the fire and a large sharp knife.

In silence, Abraham and Isaac climbed the mountain. He was sure that he was going to have to sacrifice his son. Isaac, as yet, had no idea of the turmoil in his father's mind.

"Father, we've got the wood, the fire and everything else, but where's the lamb?" Isaac asked. In anguish, Abraham looked at him. "God has got a sacrifice ready for us," he said grimly. Over and over he said to himself, "God gave us Isaac so that he would be the beginning of a new nation. He promised it. Perhaps Isaac will come back to life again." This faith kept him going.

When they reached the summit, they built an altar of stones. Abraham put the wood on top. Then he took a surprised and bewildered Isaac, tied him up and laid him on the altar. Still thinking of God's promise, and with a look of great tenderness towards his son, Abraham drew the knife. He had prepared to start the downward swing, when a powerful voice cried out, "Abraham! Abraham!" It was the angel of the Lord.

"Do not lay a hand on the boy! Now I know that you love and obey the Lord your God. You did not refuse him your only son."

Abraham almost collapsed with relief. He took Isaac off the altar and embraced him. Just a short distance away, he saw there was a ram, trapped in the thorns by its horns. God had provided a sacrifice after all and so rejoicing they returned home.

GENESIS 22:1- 14

ISAAC AND REBECCA

In time Abraham grew very old and very rich, and his son Isaac became a fine young man. But Isaac had no wife. Abraham was worried that Isaac might marry a local Canaanite girl. He felt sure God wanted Isaac to marry a girl who came from the same part of the country as Abraham, and where his relatives still lived.

Abraham explained the problem to his oldest, most trusted servant. Then Abraham said, "Go to my homeland and try to find Isaac a wife from among my relatives."

So the servant loaded ten of Abraham's camels with presents and set off on the long journey.

It was early evening on the day he arrived at the town and the local women were filling their water jars at the well. The servant prayed to God for help. "Please, God," he said, "let Isaac's bride be the woman who will offer water for my camels to drink when I ask only for a drink for myself."

Just then a beautiful young woman came to the well carrying a water jar on her shoulder. She filled the jar and the servant asked her for a drink.

"Drink, sir," she replied and gave him some water. Then she said, "I will get your camels some water too." And she carried water to the drinking trough until there was enough for all his camels.

The servant gave her gifts of gold and asked her who she was. "My name is Rebecca," she said. "My father is Bethuel, son of Nahor."

Then the servant thanked God for guiding him, for he knew Nahor was Abraham's brother.

All now went as the servant had hoped. Rebecca's family made him welcome and listened to his story. They asked Rebecca if she would marry Isaac and she agreed. Then the servant gave Rebecca and her family many valuable gifts, and she went with him to Canaan.

When Isaac saw Rebecca he fell in love with her and their marriage was a very happy one.

GENESIS 24

"I saw Rebecca coming out with her water-jar on her shoulder. She went down to the spring and drew water, and I said to her, 'Will you please give me a drink?' At once she lowered her jar from her shoulder and said, 'Drink; and I shall also water your camels.'"
Genesis 24:45–46

THE SONS OF ISAAC

After many years, Rebecca had twin sons. Before they were born she seemed to feel them fighting inside her. She asked God why this was.

God said, "Your sons will become two nations and the first son will become the second one's servant."

The first to be born was covered with red hair. They called him Esau. The second son was born holding on to Esau's heel, and he was called Jacob.

Esau became a hunter. But Jacob was quieter and preferred staying at home. Isaac loved Esau more than Jacob. But Rebecca loved Jacob.

One day when Esau came home hungry he found Jacob cooking a stew.

"Let me have some, I'm starved," exclaimed Esau.

"All right, but give me your birthright in exchange," said Jacob. Esau agreed to this at once.

Much later, when their father Isaac was old and nearly blind he called for Esau and said, "Kill a deer and bring me its meat cooked as I like it. Then I shall give you the blessing due to an eldest son from his father, for I am old and cannot live much longer."

Esau went off to hunt. But Rebecca had overheard Isaac and planned to win Jacob the blessing.

She told Jacob to kill two goats and she cooked the meat as Isaac liked it. Then she disguised Jacob in Esau's clothes and covered his hands with goatskin gloves to make them feel like Esau's hairy hands.

Jacob went in Isaac's room saying, "Here is your food, Father."

"Who are you?" asked the old man.

"Esau, your first-born." Jacob answered.

But the old man was suspicious and said, "Let me feel you."

Then he said, "Your voice is Jacob's yet your hands are Esau's."

Isaac decided it really was Esau, so he gave Jacob the blessing and made him master over his brother.

GENESIS 25:21–34; 27:1–40

JACOB AND RACHEL

Esau hated his brother so deeply for cheating him out of his rights that he planned to kill Jacob. But their mother Rebecca learned about the plan and warned Jacob to escape.

"Go and stay with your Uncle Laban," she urged. So Jacob set off north to the town of Harran.

As he came near Harran, Jacob met some shepherds by a well. He asked one of them if he knew of Laban.

"Yes," the man replied and he pointed to a girl nearby. "That is his daughter, Rachel."

Rachel took Jacob home to her father, and Laban made a great fuss of Jacob and invited him to stay.

Jacob helped Laban with his sheep for a month. Then Laban said, "Just because you're a relative, that's no reason why I shouldn't pay you for your work. What do you want?"

"I will work for you for seven years if you will let me marry Rachel," said Jacob. For he had fallen in love with the beautiful girl.

Laban agreed. But secretly he wanted Jacob to marry Rachel's elder sister Leah. For in Laban's country the elder sister always got married first.

After seven years Jacob said to Laban, "I've kept my part of our bargain. Now let me marry Rachel."

So Laban held a wedding feast. But that night he brought Jacob Leah, not Rachel. Jacob did not know, because it was dark. Next morning he found out and was angry.

Laban calmed him by saying, "In a week's time you can marry Rachel too, if you promise to stay here and work for seven more years."

So Jacob agreed, and he married Rachel as well.

After seven more years, Jacob wanted to go home to Canaan.

"Don't go," begged Laban. "Your work has helped to make me rich. Ask anything you want, but stay."

"All right," agreed Jacob. "I'll stay if you give me all your spotted, speckled and black sheep."

In that way he built up his own flocks and in six years grew rich. This made Laban so jealous, that Jacob thought Laban might take his flocks from him. So he took his wives and children and his flocks and left secretly.

GENESIS **27**:41–46 TO **31**: 1–21

JACOB'S RETURN

It was three days before Laban heard the news of his wily son-in-law's departure. He acted quickly. He set off with his men in pursuit but it was seven days before they caught up with Jacob.

Laban shouted at Jacob, "Why did you deceive me and take my daughters without so much as a goodbye? And why have you stolen my family idols?" Jacob was angry. Not knowing that in fact Rachel had taken the idols, he vowed he would kill anyone found with Laban's property.

Laban searched the camp but could find nothing. He even searched Rachel's tent. She pretended she was not well, but she was sitting on a saddle-bag in which she had hidden the gods. By this time Jacob had grown really angry.

"What right have you to hunt me down?" he stormed. "What have I done to you? I've worked all these years for your daughters and for your flocks."

The furious quarrel might have ended in disaster. But both men saw sense and made a pact. They set up a great pile of stones as a boundary, agreeing that neither would ever cross it to attack the other. They agreed that the Lord God would be the judge of their agreement. They sacrificed a goat to God and then sat down to eat a ceremonial meal together.

The next morning Laban kissed his daughters and grandchildren goodbye and returned home. At last Jacob – with God's help – was a free man, and now quite a rich one too. He set off for Canaan and home.

Jacob now decided he must make peace with his brother Esau. He despatched messengers to him, offering his friendship.

Some while later the messengers returned. "We met Esau and he is already on his way to meet you. He has a force of four hundred men!" The news confirmed Jacob's worst fears.

At once Jacob began to make plans. He divided his herds and his company into two groups so that, should Esau attack one group, the other might be able to escape. He then prayed to God.

The next day Jacob decided to send a present to Esau. From his herds he selected five hundred and eighty animals and divided them up into four or five small herds and sent them on ahead.

He then sent all the rest of the party ahead. He himself lingered behind.

That night a strange thing happened. As he tried to sleep, it seemed to him that a stranger suddenly appeared and picked a fight with him. Soon the two were on the ground both trying to gain the upper hand. As they fought, minutes then hours passed by, and still neither could gain the upper hand.

Slowly, Jacob began to realize that this was no ordinary man. There was something strange – even supernatural – about him.

Suddenly, as the sky grew lighter, the man freed one hand and jabbed a short, sharp punch at Jacob's hip. With a cry of pain Jacob collapsed to the ground and lay there, his hip dislocated. But still, gritting his teeth through the pain, Jacob held on grimly – determined not to let the man go.

"Let me go!" cried the stranger. But Jacob knew that this man was sent from God and he gasped, "No. Not unless you give me a blessing."

"What is your name?" asked the man. "Jacob," he answered. The stranger replied, "You will no longer be called Jacob. You have struggled with God and with men and you have won. From now on you will be called Israel." Jacob wanted to know more. "What is your name?" he asked. "Why do you want to know my name?" the man replied. Then he gave Jacob a blessing.

As the man blessed him, it all became clear to Jacob. This was God's blessing! He had so often wrestled with God in his mind – asking for protection and guidance. The fight was a sign that he must keep wrestling with God for the answers to his questions. The scheming Jacob must go. As the sun rose, he praised God, in wonder at what had happened.

GENESIS 31:22–55; 32

Jacob Meets Esau

At last news arrived that Esau and his men had been sighted. Jacob was still afraid that Esau would reject him.

As Esau approached, Jacob knelt down on the ground and bowed seven times. There was a long moment as Esau stood, looking at Jacob. Then, with a shout, he ran forward and threw his arms round his long-lost brother. Completely overcome by emotion, tears coursed down the faces of both men.

Then Esau saw the women and children approaching. "Whose are these?" he asked. "These are the children God has been good enough to give me," Jacob answered. He beckoned them forward and they came, one by one, to meet their uncle.

"And what did you mean by all the cattle you sent on ahead?" asked Esau. "They are for you, to show you that I want to be friends again," Jacob answered.

"Oh Jacob, you keep them. I have enough." Esau told him.

"No please, you take them. It means so much to me that you have forgiven me." As Jacob insisted, Esau accepted the gifts.

So, having met and talked of all that had happened since their youth, the time came for the brothers to part. Esau tried to persuade Jacob to follow him home. But Jacob could not move so quickly with children and young animals. He agreed to follow on later. Then, hugging each other once more they said their goodbyes.

Eventually Jacob, his family and his herds arrived in the land of Canaan, settling in the centre at a place called Shechem. There he bought land and set up an altar to worship God. And now he could call the Lord God, not only the God of his fathers Abraham and Isaac, but the God of Israel too.

GENESIS 33

JOSEPH

While Jacob and his family were travelling on to Canaan, Rachel gave birth to her second and Jacob's twelfth son. "Call him Benoni, 'child of my sorrow'," she said, as she knew that she was dying. Jacob buried his beloved wife and called his son Benjamin, 'son of my right hand'.

Benjamin and Joseph, his other son by Rachel, were Jacob's favourites. This made the other children jealous.

At the age of seventeen Joseph helped his brothers look after the sheep and goats. They had no time for him. In fact they hated him.

Joseph was a sneak. If the brothers were slack in their work with the herds, it got back to Jacob because Joseph told him. And to make matters worse Jacob had given his son a magnificent coat decorated in bright colours. Every time they saw it, the brothers hated Joseph more.

Things came to a head one morning when Joseph told his brothers about a vivid dream he had had. "I dreamt that all twelve of us were in the harvest field binding wheat sheaves and laying them on the ground. Mine stood up and your sheaves formed a circle and bowed down to it."

His brothers could not take this. "Who do you think you are?" they shouted at him. "Are you going to be a great king and rule over us?" Their hatred of him deepened.

Then Joseph had another dream in which the Sun, the Moon and eleven stars all bowed down to him. He told everyone in the family about it. His father was shocked. "Do you mean that one day your mother, brothers and I will bow down to you?" Jacob was saddened by his son's arrogance and the brothers could not wait to get their own back on him.

Before long, their chance came. They were out on the plain with the herds when Jacob sent Joseph out to see how they were doing. They saw his wonderful multi-coloured coat a long way off and it gave them time to hatch a plot. "Here comes the dreamer!" they jeered. "Let's kill him. If we throw his body down one of these dry wells we can pretend a wild animal killed him."

But Reuben, the eldest, pleaded for Joseph's life. "No, don't let's kill him. Throw him down a well but don't hurt him." Reuben planned to come back later and rescue him. The others agreed and Reuben left to look after the herds.

As Joseph came up, his brothers seized him, ripped off his coat and threw him down a well. Then they sat down to eat. On the horizon they could see a caravan of traders approaching. As the riders drew near, one of the brothers had an idea.

"We won't gain anything by killing our brother," he said. "Why don't we sell him to these traders as a slave?" Everyone agreed, so they hauled Joseph out of the well, hailed the caravan's leader and sold Joseph for twenty pieces of silver. The traders were on their way to Egypt where they knew they could get a good price for a healthy young man like Joseph.

As the traders rode off with their prize Reuben returned. He went to the well but it was empty. Reuben was very distressed, but his brothers went ahead with their plan. They prepared to fool their father by killing a goat and splashing the blood on Joseph's coat.

Arriving home they brought the torn, filthy and bloody garment to old Jacob. "We found this," they said. "Is it Joseph's coat?"

Jacob recognized it immediately. Nothing could console him. He wept and wept, tearing his clothes and covering himself with ashes. But the brothers were not really sorry for what they had done. At last Joseph – the main source of irritation all these years – was out of the way and their father might pay them some attention.

And so Joseph was on his way to Egypt. It may have seemed a disaster to the young man, but God had a reason for sending him there.

GENESIS 35:16–20; 37

When Joseph reached his brothers, they stripped him of the long robe with sleeves which he was wearing, picked him up, and threw him into the cistern. It was empty, with no water in it.

They had sat down to eat when, looking up, they saw an Ishmaelite caravan coming from Gilead on the way down to Egypt, with camels carrying gum tragacanth and balm and myrrh.

Genesis 37:23–24

THE PHARAOH'S DREAMS

In Egypt Joseph was sold to Potiphar, the captain of the Pharaoh's guard. He worked well and was soon put in charge of the whole household.

Joseph was a fine, handsome young man, and Potiphar's wife became infatuated with him. She told him of her feelings, but Joseph refused to have anything to do with her.

At last, in spiteful revenge, she told Potiphar that he had tried to make love to her.

Potiphar was furious – he had Joseph thrown into prison at once.

Among the other prisoners were the Pharaoh's royal baker and chief butler. It happened that one night they both had strange dreams.

The next day they told their dreams to Joseph, who knew that God would help interpret them.

The butler said his dream was about a vine with three branches from which he picked many grapes, squeezed their juice into the Pharaoh's cup, then offered the cup to the Pharaoh. Joseph told him this meant that the Pharaoh would send for him in three days and release him. Joseph then asked the butler to plead his case to the Pharaoh.

The baker was heartened by this news and told his dream. "I dreamt I was carrying three baskets of white bread on my head, but the birds flew down and ate all the bread in the top basket."

But Joseph shook his head sadly. He told the baker that this meant that in three days he would be executed on the Pharaoh's orders.

All came to pass as Joseph had foretold. But the butler forgot about Joseph.

Two years went by and the Pharaoh himself had two strange dreams.

He dreamt he saw seven fat, healthy cows climb out of the river Nile and stand peacefully cropping the grass on the bank. Then seven more cows climbed out of the water. Instead of eating the grass, they swallowed the seven fat cows; but still they looked thin. He then dreamt that he saw seven fat ears of corn growing on a stalk in a field. Then another stalk sprouted out of the ground with seven, thin dry ears of corn on it. As before with the cows, the thin corn swallowed the fat corn. Pharaoh woke up. He was frightened. What could the dreams mean?

He called all his advisers together and told them about his dreams. No one knew what they could mean. Then the Pharaoh's butler remembered Joseph, and he told the Pharaoh about him and how he had correctly foretold both his and the baker's dreams. The Pharaoh ordered Joseph's release.

Soon Joseph was standing in the presence of the king. He prayed silently to God as he listened to Pharaoh's account of his dreams. He knew immediately what they meant. "Your dreams have the same meaning," he said. "The seven fat cows and the seven ears of corn represent seven years of good weather and bumper harvests. The seven thin cows and the seven poor ears of corn represent seven years of terrible famine that will follow. The thin cows did not become fatter in your dream because the famine will be so great that it will wipe out even the memory of all the years of plenty."

Joseph then told the Pharaoh of a plan to save the country and its people. "Put somebody in charge of the country and its farming," he said. "Throughout the seven years of plenty he and his managers will collect one fifth of all the food grown and store it in the cities. Then there will be enough for everyone during the shortage of the next seven years.

Pharaoh was so impressed with Joseph's interpretation and his splendid plan, that he put him in charge of carrying it out immediately.

So Joseph took a fifth of all the country's produce during the seven years of good harvests and stored it away in silos. Joseph was only thirty years old; a very young age for such an important position. But he firmly believed God had given him the work to do and would help him.

GENESIS 39 TO 41

JOSEPH'S BROTHERS

Just as Joseph had foretold, a more unsettled period began after the seven years of good harvests. There were storms and drought, crops grew badly and harvests were poor.

Soon the Egyptians began to run out of food. "Help us, Pharaoh, we're getting hungry," they cried. "You go and ask Joseph what to do," Pharaoh told them. When the food shortage had become really severe Joseph opened up the great storehouses and sold supplies to all who needed them. His plan was a great success.

Not only Egypt, but all the surrounding countries were also suffering from famine. Before long people came from everywhere to buy grain, including Canaan where Joseph's own family were badly short of food. Joseph's father, Jacob, told ten of his sons to go to Egypt to buy grain. Benjamin stayed at home.

When the brothers arrived in Egypt they were told to go to Joseph, who directed all selling of grain to foreigners. But they did not recognize their young brother. He was clean shaven like an Egyptian and wore fine clothes and rare jewels. They bowed down before him in respect.

Joseph knew who they were immediately. In the shock of seeing them he decided not to tell them who he was. He would test them to see if they felt sorry for what they had done to him. He treated them like strangers and spoke harshly to them. Pretending he did not understand their language, he spoke to them through an interpreter. "You are spies. You have come to see how weak we are."

The brothers were horrified. "No, no," they protested. "We are not spies. We have come to buy grain. We are ten of twelve brothers. One brother is at home, the other one is dead." Joseph pretended he did not believe them. They were put in prison and questioned for three days about the family history.

On the third day he released them. "I am a Godfearing man," he said. "I will give you the chance to prove that you are honest. One of you will stay here in prison while the others return home with the grain. But you must bring back with you the youngest brother you have told me about."

The brothers were frightened and felt guilty. "We're in trouble with this man because of what we did to Joseph," they said. "It's God's way of punishing us." Joseph sat listening to them. Now he knew that they were sorry for what they had done.

But Joseph had not finished with them yet. He kept his brother, Simeon, in jail, and before the brothers set out for home he secretly put the money they had given him for the grain back into the sacks on their pack donkeys.

On the way home the brothers stopped for the night and one of them opened a sack to feed his donkey. There, on top of the grain, was the money bag. How had it got there?

The frightened group of brothers arrived home and told their father Jacob everything that had happened. When they emptied the rest of the grain sacks to show him what they had bought, out fell the other money bags! Jacob was angry and shouted at them, "Last time you went away you came back without Joseph and now you come back without Simeon. Then you tell me you want to take Benjamin, my youngest son." Jacob refused to send Benjamin back to Egypt with his brothers. He still mourned for Joseph and he was not going to let his new favourite leave his side.

GENESIS 42

Joseph's brothers came and bowed to the ground before him, and when he saw his brothers he recognized them but, pretending not to know them, he greeted them harshly.
Genesis 42:6–7

THE SILVER CUP

Jacob hoped that the famine would soon stop, and that rain and good crops would come again. But they did not. Before long all the grain the brothers had brought from Egypt was gone. So their father told them: "You will have to go to Egypt again to buy us more food."

Judah reminded him of their last visit. "You realize we will have to take Benjamin with us. The Egyptian was serious when he said, 'Don't come back without your brother.'" Jacob remembered the terms. "Why did you tell him about Benjamin?" he asked bitterly. "We had no idea he would want to see him," they replied. Judah tried to reassure his father, promising to take special care of the favourite son.

Reluctantly Jacob agreed. "Take as many gifts as we can afford," he said. "Honey, spices, balm, pistachio nuts and almonds, the best the land can provide. Take twice as much money this time, so that you can pay back what was left in your sacks."

So the brothers set off with their laden pack-donkeys. They were again presented to Joseph. He invited them to eat with him at his private house at noon. While he had gone to instruct his stewards to prepare a feast, the brothers looked at one another nervously. "Why should he want us to come to his private house? He must think we stole the money we found and is going to make us slaves."

At Joseph's palace they went straight to his household manager. "On our way back home last time," they said, "we found our money still in our sacks. We don't know how it got there. We didn't steal it. We've brought it back as well as more money

to pay for more grain." Joseph's manager looked at them kindly. "Don't worry," he said, "that money must have been a gift from God, because our books say that the grain was paid for!"

Joseph arrived at his palace at noon. He greeted his brothers and was especially kind to Benjamin. Simeon was released from prison and joined them. The brothers began to enjoy the feast.

But when they were ready to leave, Joseph told his steward to fill their sacks with all the grain they could carry and once again to put back the money that had been paid. And, on top of Benjamin's sack, Joseph's own silver cup was placed.

After they had left, Joseph ordered his men to pursue the brothers. Joseph's men soon overtook the caravan and brought it to a halt.

"Who do you take us for?" the brothers demanded. "We've already tried to return the money we found. Do you think we would then go back and steal from your master again?" But they had to allow their sacks to be searched, from the oldest brother down to the youngest. Of course Joseph's men found the money in the top of each sack, and last of all, when Benjamin's sack was opened, out fell Joseph's silver cup. In despair, the brothers reloaded the sacks and headed back to the city.

Joseph was waiting for them. He pretended to be angry. "What can we say to prove we are innocent?" they pleaded. "This must be God's punishment for our evil past. Take us as your slaves." But Joseph said, "I'll only take the one who stole my cup." Desperately, Judah spoke up "Please, don't take Benjamin. If you made him a slave his father would die of sorrow. Let me stay as your slave instead."

Joseph ordered his attendants out of the room so that he could be alone with his brothers. Then he broke down in tears. "I am your brother Joseph!" he said. His brothers were dumbfounded.

"Don't feel guilty about what happened," Joseph said. "It is God's plan. He has given me this position so that I can look after our people in these hard times. He wants us all to stay alive because we are the beginning of a great nation – his people. I want you to go home and fetch our father and come and live here with me." Then he kissed them all.

GENESIS 43–45: 1–15

Life in Egypt

Before long everyone in Joseph's household knew that he had been reunited with his family. The Egyptians were overjoyed for him. When Pharaoh heard, he was pleased too. He insisted that Joseph send for his father and promised he would be given all the privileges of an honoured citizen.

Joseph's brothers returned to Canaan and told Jacob the good news. He was overjoyed to hear that Jospeh was alive. They set off for Egypt at once.

On the way they stopped at Beersheba, on the borders of Canaan, to offer sacrifices to God. That night God spoke to Jacob in a dream. "Do not be afraid to go to Egypt, for I promise that your family will be the beginning of a great nation and I will bring your descendants back to their homeland. You, Jacob, will die in Egypt."

In time they arrived in Egypt. When he saw his father, Joseph was overcome by emotion. They fell into one another's arms and wept with joy. Pharaoh treated them well and gave them much valuable land on which to live and rear their livestock.

While Joseph's family settled into their new home, Joseph was kept busy with affairs of state. The famine was still raging and the people of Egypt were rapidly using up the grain from the city storehouses. Until now, people had paid for the grain, but before long most families had no money left. They pleaded: "You must let us have grain or we shall die!" So Joseph decided to take livestock in exchange for the grain. The seven years of famine dragged on and eventually there were no cattle left to exchange. So Joseph accepted land in payment, until all the cultivated land in Egypt belonged to the Pharaoh.

However, Joseph soon realized that this policy would not be good for Egypt. When better times came, the people would have no land to cultivate to support themselves. So Joseph devised a new plan. He leased the land back to the people, announcing, "You may cultivate the leased land and I will give you seed to sow. When it is harvested, you may keep four-fifths of the crops to live on and to sow again. The other fifth must be paid to Pharaoh."

Joseph's decision changed the whole way of life in Egypt for a long time. It led to a strong and wealthy ruling family but also saved the lives of the Egyptian farmers.

Jacob lived for another seventeen years. He saw his family become well established and prosperous in the new country. It grew into a huge tribe. When Jacob died at a great age, the whole nation went into mourning for seventy days.

Some time later Joseph took his brothers into his confidence. "Soon I am going to die," he said, "but God has promised that in his own time he will take our family out of Egypt, back to the Promised Land."

When Joseph died, his body was embalmed in the Egyptian way and kept as a treasured possession.

Jacob's family lived very well in Egypt. After Joseph's death, Pharaoh allowed them to stay on as a separate tribe, and they settled in a land called Goshen. They grew in numbers, and adapted well to the settled life of Egypt.

Three hundred peaceful years passed. Then a Pharaoh came to the throne who thought it was dangerous to have such a large and prosperous immigrant community living among his own people. At any time they could ally themselves to a foreign power and overthrow the government.

Pharaoh had large building projects in mind, and here was a ready-made labour force. So instead of allowing the Israelites the freedom to work their own land as before, he passed new laws making them slaves to the Egyptians.

Building in Egypt was done entirely by hand, using thousands of workers. It was tough work for even the fittest. The work-gangs were driven by task-masters who flogged anyone who slackened. Life became unbearable for the Israelites.

GENESIS 45:16–28 TO 50; EXODUS 1:6–11

"These Israelites have become too many and too strong for us. We must take steps to ensure that they increase no further;"
Exodus 1:9–10

MOSES IN THE BULRUSHES

Even under the cruel treatment of Egyptian rule, the Israelites continued to flourish and grow. The Pharaoh decided to take more drastic action. He appointed two Egyptan women to help as midwives to the Hebrews. He ordered them to kill every baby boy they delivered. Bravely, the women refused. They feared God and they would do nothing to harm his chosen people.

Angrily, Pharaoh issued orders to his people. All baby boys born to Israelites must be thrown into the Nile and drowned. The Israelites were angry and horrified at this new order. Parents tried to hide their babies from the authorities, but many were drowned.

One Hebrew mother had a baby son who was so beautiful that she could not bear to let him die. For three months she hid him; but she knew she could not go on hiding him for ever.

So the mother wove a tiny boat out of reeds, and waterproofed it with tar. Then she laid her child tenderly in the boat, and set it among the reeds that grew by the river. The baby's sister hid nearby, and watched to see what happened.

Soon the Pharaoh's own daughter, a princess, came to the river to bathe. As she walked with her maids she glimpsed the reed boat, and wondered what it could be. The princess sent one of her maids to fetch it. When the princess peered inside, the baby started to cry. He was so lovely and helpless that she felt sorry for him. "This must be one of the Hebrew's children," she said.

Then Miriam ran from her hiding place. "Shall I find a Hebrew woman to look after the child for you?" she asked.

"Yes, do that," the princess replied. So the baby's delighted sister rushed home to fetch her mother.

"Take this child and nurse him for me," commanded the princess.

The mother obeyed. She was thrilled to have saved her baby, although she knew that she must soon give him up for good.

When the baby was older the princess adopted him, and he grew up in her palace. She called him Moses, which sounds like a Hebrew word meaning 'to draw out'. For she said, "I drew him out of the water."

EXODUS 1:12–22 TO 2:1–10

She conceived and bore a son, and when she saw what a fine child he was, she kept him hidden for three months. Unable to conceal him any longer, she got a rush basket for him, made it watertight with pitch and tar, laid him in it, and placed it among the reeds by the bank of the Nile.
Exodus 2:2–3

She noticed the basket among the reeds and sent her slave-girl to bring it. When she opened it, there was the baby, it was crying, and she was moved with pity for it. "This must be one of the Hebrew children," she said. Exodus 2:5–6

49

THE BURNING BUSH

The Egyptians who raised Moses never imagined he would become a great Hebrew leader. But he grew up knowing he was an Israelite – a Hebrew descended from Israel, the name God gave to Jacob. Moses was aware of how cruelly the Egyptians treated his people. One day he saw an Egyptian beating an Israelite slave. In anger, Moses killed the Egyptian and fled before the crime was discovered.

He travelled on until he came to a desert land where he worked as a shepherd for a man called Jethro. He soon settled into his new life and married one of Jethro's daughters, Zipporah.

One day, Moses was alone with his sheep, when he noticed that a bush was on fire. It burned and burned, yet never seemed to burn up.

Moses walked closer, his eyes wide with amazement. Then a voice from the bush called: "Moses, Moses."

Moses shook with fear and covered his face with his hands, for he guessed it was God's voice. Timidly he replied, "Here I am."

God said, "I have seen the misery of my people in Egypt. I have come to lead them away to a fertile land. You must go with the elders of the people to see Pharaoh and tell him to let you take the Israelites out into the desert to make sacrifices to me."

Now Moses was no braver than most of us. "I'm not the man for that," he objected. "No one will believe that God has told me to do it."

But God insisted. And he gave Moses the power to perform miracles so that he could prove that God had sent him.

First he told Moses to throw his walking staff on the ground. As he did so it became a poisonous snake, writhing in the sand. When Moses picked it up, it became a staff again.

Then God told Moses to put his hand into his robe. When he brought it out it was diseased with leprosy. When he put his hand back in his robe it was healed. God continued: "If the Israelites do not believe you after these two signs, pour some water from the river Nile on the ground and it will turn into blood."

Even then Moses stammered excuses. "P-P-Please, I d-d-don't speak well. S-S-Send someone else."

God began to grow angry. He snapped, "Your brother Aaron speaks well. He can do the talking if you cannot manage."

Then God promised that Moses could safely return to Egypt without fear of arrest.

EXODUS 2 TO 4:1–17

The Lord said, "I have witnessed the misery of my people in Egypt and have heard them crying out because of their oppressors. I know what they are suffering and have come down to rescue them from the power of the Egyptians and to bring them up out of that country into a fine, broad land, a land flowing with milk and honey."
Exodus 3:7–8

50

51

THE TEN PLAGUES

With God's special commission still echoing in his mind, Moses went back to his father-in-law and asked if he could return to Egypt. Jethro gave his blessing and Moses set off with his wife and sons. As God had foretold, Moses met his brother Aaron in the desert and explained to him everything that God had told him.

When they arrived in Egypt, they called a meeting of all the elders of the Hebrew families. Aaron acted as Moses' spokesman and Moses performed the miracles God had shown him. Seeing Moses' power and hearing God's promise to rescue them, the elders were overjoyed and happily accepted the brothers as their leaders.

When the time came, it took a year of disasters to accomplish God's plan, a year in which Moses and Aaron were continually put to the test.

To begin with, Moses and Aaron, full of confidence in God's power, appeared before Pharaoh and told him of God's message. "The God of Israel says, 'Let my people go, so that they can hold a festival in the desert to honour me.'" Pharaoh refused.

"Who is this God that I should take any notice of him? I will not let the people go," he shouted. "Your people are obviously not working hard enough if you have time for festivals."

Pharaoh decided to make things even harder for the Hebrews. One of the slaves' jobs was to make bricks for building. Normally they were given straw to mix with the clay before the bricks were baked. Pharaoh now ordered the slaves to find their own straw, but to make exactly the same number of bricks each day.

In desperation a deputation of foremen came to Pharaoh and pleaded with him to be reasonable. "If you have time to go and worship your God," Pharaoh replied, "you're obviously not working hard enough. Get on with it."

The miserable foreman turned on Moses and

Aaron. "We hope God punishes you for what you've done!" they said bitterly. "Because of you, Pharaoh hates us and now has an excuse to kill us."

Moses was shocked. Silently he prayed to God. "How can you do this to your people? In sending me to Pharaoh you have made things even harder than before."

But God was patient with Moses. "Wait and see what I will do," he said. "In the end Pharaoh will drive you out of the land."

So Moses went back to the elders and tried to encourage them by telling them what God was going to do. But they were so dispirited they found it hard to believe Moses.

Summoning all their courage and faith Moses and Aaron asked for a second audience with the Pharaoh. Once more they told the king that they wanted to take all their belongings and travel three days into the desert to worship God. To prove their authority to be God's spokesmen, Aaron threw his staff down, as God had shown Moses. Immediately, it became a snake. But Egyptian courts were used to such signs. Pharaoh called his sorcerers, who by the skilled use of magic, were able to do similar things. Their staffs, too, appeared to become snakes and for one terrible moment the palace floor was crawling with them. As everyone watched open mouthed, Aaron's snake swallowed up all the others. But still Pharaoh would not change his mind.

God now told Moses to meet the king by the river Nile the next morning. As Pharaoh and his court appeared, Aaron stepped up to him and said, "Now God will show you who he is by what he does to your land." He raised the staff in his hand and brought it down hard on the surface of the river. Slowly, the Nile turned blood red. Soon the water was so polluted that all the fish died. The court sorcerers, anxious about their jobs, convinced Pharaoh that they could do the same thing by magic. So Pharaoh remained stubborn. But for seven days the water of the Nile was undrinkable.

This disaster was just the first of a series. Soon, millions of frogs left the rivers and canals and hopped about the land. People found them everywhere. Once again, Pharaoh's magicians made light of the problem, but Pharaoh was beginning to feel uneasy. This God was a powerful enemy. "All right,"

he said to Moses, "Ask your God to take the frogs away and I'll let you go."

Moses prayed and God did as Moses asked. The frogs on the land died. But Pharaoh again refused to listen to Moses and Aaron.

God told Moses that Aaron should strike the ground with his staff. As Aaron did so swarms of maggots spread over the land, covering animals and people like dust. The people itched, and scratched themselves. This time the magicians were beaten;

they could not make maggots appear by magic. But Pharaoh was still stubborn.

To add to the misery caused by the maggots swarms of flies now infested Egypt, except for Goshen where the Israelites lived. Pharaoh tried to persuade Moses to agree to make his sacrifices in Egypt, but Moses refused. "Our sacrifices of animals offend your people," he said. "We would be in danger of being stoned by them. We must go into the desert." Pharaoh finally relented. He said that the Israelites could go into the desert, but not very far, if Moses made the wretched flies go away. Moses prayed to God and the flies went. But Pharaoh broke his word again.

By now Egypt was in a very bad way. God promised, through Moses and Aaron, that there would be more plagues. An epidemic spread like

wildfire through the Egyptian cattle and many of them became sick and died. The Israelite livestock remained perfectly healthy, showing that God was protecting Israel. Yet still Pharaoh was stubborn and refused to let the people go.

Finally, infection spread to the people. Moses and Aaron, on God's instructions, took handfuls of ash and threw it up in the air. As the dust settled, people and animals became badly infected with boils. Pharaoh still refused to listen.

The next warning God gave, included a way out for those Egyptians who believed he would carry out his threats. Through the two brothers, he warned of a great hail storm, with stones so big they could kill. Some of the Egyptians were sensible and took the warning seriously. They shut up their animals and rushed indoors. Others took no notice.

The storm was indeed the worst Egypt had ever known. The flax and barley crops, nearly ready for harvesting, were flattened by hailstones.

Pharaoh was beginning to get the point. He told Moses: "I have done wrong, so have my people. Your God is in the right. Ask him to stop this awful storm and your people can go."

Moses knew that Pharaoh did not yet truly fear God. But he did as Pharaoh asked. As he prayed, the storm stopped. Pharaoh then tried to negotiate with the Israelites. "Just who is going on this holiday?" he asked. "All of us," replied Moses. "I knew it!" burst out Pharaoh. "You are planning to revolt, not worship. I will not allow it."

"Then see what the Lord will do," replied Moses.

The Egyptian wheat crop had survived the storms because it was not ripe. Just as it became ready for harvest a great cloud of locusts, carried on an east wind, hit Egypt. The wheat fields were blackened by them. They ate everything the hail had left. Egypt's economy was in ruins. Pharaoh pleaded for the locusts to be removed. When they were, he sent Moses and Aaron away again.

So God plunged the whole land into darkness. A thick dust storm blanketed out the sun's light. The Egyptians could see nothing for three whole days, and they were very frightened. Pharaoh tried one last ploy. The Israelites could all go into the desert, but they were to leave their cattle behind. Moses refused. It was their privilege, he said, to choose their own animals for sacrifice. The livestock must go with them. By this time Pharaoh was beside himself with anger. He shouted at Moses, "Get out of my sight or I'll kill you!"

"Don't worry," replied Moses, "I will go, and you will not see me again, ever!"

EXODUS *4:18–31* TO **10**

THE PASSOVER

The terrible year of disasters had left Egypt near to ruin. Her crops were wasted, her livestock sick and the people miserable and afraid. It was a high price to pay for resisting the God of Israel. But the year left Pharaoh more stubborn and more determined than ever to keep the slaves. It had become an obsession with him. He was king, he would not obey his slaves' God.

The Israelite people were now ready, longing to leave Egypt for their own territory. The time had come for God to free his people; no Pharaoh had any power to stop them. So God told Moses about the last great disaster that was to befall the Egyptians and their Pharaoh.

Moses and Aaron then called the elders of the community together and outlined God's plan. They now knew that these men spoke God's words and were to be trusted and obeyed. Soon individual families were given their instructions and there was great excitement as the chosen day was whispered from family to family.

First, the people were to go to their Egyptian neighbours and ask to borrow gold, jewellery and clothes for their festival. Then, on the tenth of the month they were to prepare for the great escape. There would be no time for proper preparations for the desert journey, so each family was to select a healthy young sheep or kid to be slaughtered for their evening meal. But it was no normal dinner, as each mother and father explained to the children. The meat was to be roasted with bitter herbs to remind them how much they had suffered in Egypt. With the meal the families were to have bread made quickly, without any yeast. The rest of the dough should be put in their baking pans ready for the journey. Before the meal began each family had to be packed, ready to set off at a moment's notice.

By the evening of the fourteenth, the community at Goshen was buzzing with suppressed excitement as the families began their preparations. Each father took a knife and slit the throat of his lamb or kid, holding it over a bowl to catch the blood. Dipping a branch from a hyssop bush into the blood he solemnly brushed it over the beam above the door and down the doorposts. Then, the family went inside, shut their door and began to prepare the meal. The strange action was to save the lives of their sons.

Meanwhile, in the rest of Egypt the fateful night began quietly. No one suspected anything unusual. Pharaoh waited in his palace. He had been warned of God's terrible last sign but he would not believe it, neither would he change his mind.

Midnight came and suddenly a terrible wailing began in the Egyptian city. In family after family, death struck the eldest son! God had sent his angel of death into the land. No Egyptian family was spared. Even Pharaoh's son and heir died that night. The first-born male animals lay dead too. Only those in the houses with blood on their doorposts were safe. Not one Israelite son died, the angel passed over their houses, leaving them to eat their last meal in Egypt in safety.

Standing by the bedside of his dead son, Pharaoh knew that he could resist God no longer. He called Moses and Aaron to him in the middle of the night and stormed, "Get out of my country. Take your families, your cattle, everything! But go *now*! But pray for me," he added in his misery. "I have sinned." The Egyptian people pleaded with the Israelites too. "Please go," they cried. "Leave the country before we all die."

The people of Israel were ready. Moses and Aaron gave the word at once and the whole tribe set out into the desert to return to the land God had promised them. The Israelites had a long way to go and many adventures and difficulties would come their way. But as they left Egypt their spirits were high. God had set them free. Whatever happened, they were no longer slaves.

EXODUS 11 TO 13:1–18

Crossing the Red Sea

When the Israelites set off into the desert, God gave them a sign to show that he was leading them on their historic journey. In the day they could clearly see a great column of cloud, like a pillar, at the head of the march. At night this became a bright column of fire.

The Israelites followed the column to the Red Sea or Sea of Reeds, part of the Bitter Lakes near their old home. But the escape was not as easy as they had hoped. As soon as they had left, Pharaoh regretted his decision. He and his people had lost their slaves. He decided to force them to return. The cruel ruler mobilized his armies and set off at the head of his unit of expert charioteers.

Meanwhile, Moses, at God's command, camped between a range of mountains and the edge of the Sea of Reeds. While they rested and ate, lookouts paced the heights above. Suddenly they spotted the Egyptian forces in hot pursuit.

This was to be the Israelites' first test of faith in God. But instead of showing trust, they panicked and accused Moses and Aaron of throwing away their lives. Moses quietened them and said, "Don't be afraid. The Lord will fight for us."

Then God said to Moses, "Take your staff and raise it high over the sea." The Israelites crowded round as their leader stood on a rock and held his staff over the waters. As he did so, the pillar of cloud came between the Egyptians and the Israelites, creating a screen so that the army could not attack. All through the night Moses held his staff high and the Israelites noticed a steady east wind blowing across the water in front of them. By morning the water had drawn back to leave a roadway across the sea. At Moses' order the whole nation marched across the dry sea bed.

As morning came, the Egyptians broke through the barrier of cloud. As the last Israelite family left the marshy area the Egyptians were in sight directly behind them. But God was firmly in control. The Egyptians' chariot wheels became stuck in the soft sea bed. While they were held up, God ordered Moses to raise his staff again. This time the water returned to its normal level with a mighty roar, catching the whole army and destroying it.

This miraculous escape restored the Israelites' faith in God and their confidence in Moses.

EXODUS 13:20–22 TO 14

Manna from Heaven

The Israelites had escaped from the cruel Egyptians. But they faced new difficulties. Back in the fertile farmlands of Egypt they had had enough to eat and drink. Now they found themselves on the edge of the dusty, mountainous deserts of Sinai where food and water were scarce.

For three days after crossing the Red Sea the Israelites found nothing to drink. Then when they found water it tasted bitter.

The people stopped being grateful to Moses for helping them to escape from Egypt. Instead, they began blaming him for their troubles. "What can we drink?" they demanded. So, with God's help Moses found a way to make the water drinkable, and for a while the refugees stopped complaining.

Next they discovered a shady oasis with palm trees and wells, but beyond that stretched more pitiless desert. Six weeks after leaving Egypt the Israelites were very hungry, and very unhappy.

"God might as well have killed us in Egypt. At least we had plenty to eat there. Now you seem to have dragged us out here just so we can die from hunger," they grumbled.

But God said to Moses, "I shall rain food from heaven. Each day the people can gather enough for that day. On the sixth day of the week they will gather enough for two days."

That evening there was a flutter of wings, and scores of quail landed around the camp. Tired after a long flight, the small birds were easy to catch, and tasty to eat.

And that was not all. Next morning, people noticed that the ground was covered with tiny flakes that looked like hoarfrost.

"What is it?" they asked Moses.

"It must be the bread God has given you to eat," he replied.

The strange food tasted like honey-bread and the people called it manna, which means 'what is it?'

The Israelites gathered the manna quickly, for they found that it vanished as the sun grew hot.

Every day there was just enough manna to last each person till night. But on the sixth day there was enough for two days.

The people asked Moses why this was so. He explained, "Because God has made the seventh day of the week a rest day. We must do no work on that day, and keep it holy." (This story helps to explain why Jews and Christians set aside one day a week for worshipping God.)

For the next forty years the Israelites trudged with all their belongings from one waterhole to the next. Wherever they went, God sent manna to feed them.

EXODUS 15:22–27 TO 16

The Lord spoke to Moses: "I have heard the complaints of the Israelites. Say to them: Between dusk and dark you will have flesh to eat and in the morning bread in plenty."

WATER FROM THE ROCK

The Israelites had plenty to eat as they journeyed on. But water became scarce as the desert landscape changed to the rocky foothills of the Sinai mountain range. One evening, as they pitched camp at a place called Rephidim, the Israelites began to complain again. There was no water for miles.

"Have you brought us all this way just to let us die?" they demanded of Moses. "Why must you keep complaining?" he asked. "Are you trying to test God?" But the people were so angry that Moses began to fear for his life. He went away and prayed to God for help.

Once more God told Moses how he could find water. He was to gather the leaders and take them into the mountains. There he would find a particular rock which he was to strike with his staff. He found the rock and as he struck it a spring of water gushed out and ran down the slope. The men were amazed. There was now enough water for everyone. God had shown yet again that he could be trusted.

One day, during their stay at Rephidim there was a shout from the lookouts. A hostile tribe, the Amalekites, were about to attack the camp.

Moses made hasty battle plans. He ordered Joshua, his chief of defence, to fight the Amalekites at dawn the next day. "Meanwhile," he told Joshua, "I will go to the top of the mountain to pray." The camp was a bustle of activity as Joshua organized his men. He formed them into ranks and told them the plan of action.

By dawn the Israelites were in position and Moses stood on a rocky peak overlooking the field of battle. Joshua's forces attacked and the Amalekites fought back. They were a tough, warlike people and the battle was fierce. But things went well for the Israelites. High above them they could see Moses, arms aloft and staff in hand, praying to God for victory.

So long as Moses held his arms aloft Joshua's forces gradually gained the upper hand. By sundown the Israelites had beaten the Amalekite army.

The victory boosted the spirits of the Israelite community. That night there was singing and dancing as the battered but cheerful heroes returned to the camp. They gave praise to God for saving them from their enemies.

The Israelites stayed at Rephidim for some time, and while they were there, Moses was reunited with his wife, Zipporah. She had travelled with his sons and his father-in-law, Jethro, all the way from Midian, having heard of the remarkable escape from Egypt. It was a happy reunion for the family.

Moses greatly respected his father-in-law and lost no time in telling him everything that had happened since the time he had left Midian to return to Egypt. Although he was not an Israelite, Jethro believed in Moses' God and was full of praises to God for the way he had rescued and looked after his son-in-law's people.

Moses as their leader, was also the Israelites' final authority on matters of law. Anyone with any kind of dispute, however small, brought it before him for judgement. Moses sat as judge and jury from dawn to dusk. It was exhausting work, and time was often wasted trying to sort out petty squabbles.

When Jethro saw this, he was astounded. "Why do you wear yourself out like this?" he asked. "I have to," Moses replied, simply. "The people need to know how God wants them to act in their daily lives, so they come to me. I tell them what God's laws and commands are."

Jethro was the leader of the Midianite tribe and he now gave Moses some advice. He said, "I'm sure that it is right to represent your people before God and teach them his laws, but you can't do it all. Appoint God-fearing, trustworthy men to act as judges over the minor disputes. If they have a serious or difficult case, then they can refer it to you. In that way everyone's arguments will be settled, and you won't be burdened with everyday problems."

Jethro's advice made sense and Moses was sure it had God's approval. He picked out people he could trust and established a system of permanent judges, each one over ten, fifty, a hundred or a thousand people.

Jethro stayed with the Israelites until Moses had set up his new legal system and then returned to his home in Midian.

Moses then ordered the people to pack everything together for the next stage of the journey. They were headed for Mount Sinai, the Holy Mountain, which marked the end of the first stage of their journey.

Two months after they had set off from Egypt, the great sprawling procession arrived in the mountains. They were to stay there for a whole year, during which time there were to be some dramatic events that would affect the whole future of the Israelite nation.

EXODUS 17 TO 18

The people became so thirsty there that they raised an outcry against Moses: "Why have you brought us out of Egypt with our children and our herds to let us die of thirst?"
Exodus 17:3

MOSES ON MOUNT SINAI

The Israelites set up camp at the foot of Mount Sinai and Moses climbed to the mountain's peak. On the mountain, God was going to establish a binding agreement with the people of Israel that would make them a special nation. He said to Moses, "I will make a solemn agreement with you all. The whole of the Earth is mine, but you will be my chosen people. Your nation must keep my commandments and dedicate themselves to me only."

Moses returned to the people waiting below. He called the leaders together and explained what God had promised. They vowed, on behalf of the people, to keep their part of the agreement. "We will do everything God has said," they told Moses.

The old man returned to the mountain top and told God of their promises, while the Israelites waited expectantly below. So God told Moses how to prepare for the dramatic moment when he would reveal his mighty presence to them. The Israelites were to wash their clothes as a sign of making themselves clean and pure before God. They were to make a boundary around the base of the holy mountain which the Israelites should not cross. If they did so they would die. Then they were to wait for a special sign to show that God was with them.

By the third day, everyone was ready and dressed in clean clothes. They waited with a mixture of excitement, curiosity and fear.

Suddenly a crash of thunder rolled out, louder than anything they had ever heard. Lightning flashed and a vast, dark cloud descended on the mountain top. A majestic trumpet blared and echoed around the mountainside. Everyone in the camp shook with fear, from the youngest child to the toughest soldier.

Then Moses led the people out of the camp to the foot of the mountain, just below the marked boundary. By now the whole mountain was covered with clouds of smoke, showing that God's presence was there.

The great trumpet fanfare grew even louder and Moses cried out to God. The Lord answered him in a voice of thunder. Then Moses went up the mountain into the presence of Jehovah. He took Aaron with him but the people dared not approach the mountain. "You tell us what God says," they pleaded. "If God speaks to us we will die."

EXODUS 19

THE TEN COMMANDMENTS

High on the mountain, the Lord gave his commands to Moses. These commands became the laws by which the Israelites had to live if they were to remain God's chosen people. His laws did not just cover worship, but also the way people had to treat one another. Every part of their life fell under God's rules. They were contained in ten guidelines on how to behave. These have become the basis of law for many societies ever since.

The commandments were simple, yet profound. The Israelites were to worship no god other than God himself. They should not make idols or statues to worship, or misuse the name of God. Every seventh day should be kept as a rest day, dedicated to God and his worship.

Children were to respect and obey their parents. Murder was wrong, and so were adultery and stealing. Lies were not to be told against others and no one should be jealous of anyone because of what they owned.

If the people lived by these rules, treating their fellows with love and fairness, and continued to worship the Lord who made them, they would prosper.

God also gave Moses more detailed instructions on how people should live from day to day. Worship must be simple; altars were to be made from earth or uncut stone, not grand affairs of silver or gold.

The Israelites could be quick-tempered and violent in their quarrels, so punishments for violence and murder were to be strict. Murder and a number of other serious crimes carried the death penalty. For assault that caused injury, compensation had to be given.

There were laws dealing with injury, theft and damage to property, and also those to protect young girls from rape or seduction. Foreigners were not to be ill-treated and the poor were not to be made to pay high interest rates by moneylenders.

God told the Israelites to set aside part of their corn, wine and olive oil as an offering and that each first-born son should be dedicated to him. First-born cattle and sheep should be offered as a sacrifice to God.

God was determined that the people should live alongside one another in peace. He condemned the spreading of false rumours about innocent people, and all forms of bribery. His people must be responsible in their actions and always ready to help others.

God told Moses the annual festivals he wanted his nation to keep. They were the Feast of the Passover, which celebrated the nation's deliverance from Egypt by God, the Festival of Harvest and the Festival of Firstfruits, to be held in the autumn when the grapes were picked and collected for storage.

If his people were faithful, there would be blessings too. God would fight for them in battle, they would not be short of food or water, neither would they be stricken with diseases. The women of the community would have no difficulty in bearing children and people would live to a good old age.

When Moses came down the mountain, the Israelites fell silent as he gave them these instructions. Having seen the power of God the people answered immediately: "We will do everything God has said." Moses then wrote down the commandments as a permanent record.

The next morning Moses built a special altar. On it he set twelve rocks, one for each of the tribes of Israel. Animals were killed for sacrifice on the altar. Moses took their blood and sprinkled half of it on the sides of the altar to signify God's part of the agreement. He splashed he other half over the people as a sign to show that they had made their promise too.

The ceremony over, Moses took Aaron, two of Aaron's sons and seventy of the Israelite leaders up the Holy Mountain with him. There they were given a privilege only a very few people in history have ever had. They were granted a vision of God. It seemed that beneath him stretched a dazzling pavement of sapphires, blue as a summer sky.

Then Aaron and the leaders rejoined the Israelites, full of everything they had seen and heard. But Moses returned to the peak where he was to stay in God's presence for forty days and nights. As he climbed, a dense cloud covered the mountain again. From below it looked as if a fire was raging on the peak.

God gave Moses many more laws. The laws were engraved on stone tablets. "These tablets contain all the laws that I have given for the instruction of the people," God told Moses.

But at the very moment when Moses was sealing the agreement with God, the Israelites had begun to break it.

EXODUS 20 TO 24

When all the people saw how it thundered and the lightning flashed, when they heard the trumpet sound and saw the mountain in smoke, they were afraid and trembled. They stood at a distance and said to Moses, "Speak to us yourself and we will listen; but do not let God speak to us or we shall die." Moses answered, "Do not be afraid. God has come only to test you, so that the fear of him may remain with you and preserve you from sinning." So the people kept their distance, while Moses approached the dark cloud where God was.
Exodus 20:18–21

The Ten Commandments

1. *Do not worship any other gods but the Lord your God.*

2. *Do not make any statues or any likenesses that is in heaven above, or on the earth below, or in the water under the earth, and do not bow down to them in worship.*

3. *Do not misuse the name of the Lord your God.*

4. *Remember to keep the Sabbath day holy. You have six days to work; but the seventh day is when you must rest.*

5. *Honour your father and your mother.*

6. *Do not commit murder.*

7. *Do not be unfaithful to your husband or wife.*

8. *Do not steal.*

9. *Do not speak falsely against your neighbour.*

10. *Do not be envious of your neighbour — whether it concerns his wife, slave, animals, or anything that belongs to him.*

THE GOLDEN CALF

Moses stayed so long on the mountain that the people below grew impatient. They went to Moses' brother Aaron and said, "Make us a god as our leader, for we don't know what can have happened to Moses."

To keep them quiet Aaron agreed. He melted down their gold earrings, then moulded and cut the gold into the shape of a calf. The people were thrilled. They said, "This is the god that saved us from Egypt."

The next day the Israelites placed offerings before the calf. Then they held a wild party.

Meanwhile, on the mountain, God told Moses, "Your people have disobeyed me and worship an idol."

Moses choked with anger to think his people had turned their backs on God after all they had promised. Clutching the slabs bearing the Ten Commandments, he stormed down the mountainside.

Yes! There they all were; a drunken crowd, dancing and singing around a golden calf.

Moses furiously raised the heavy stone slabs above his head, and smashed them on the ground.

Stunned silence followed. Scared and guilty, the Israelites hung their heads and meekly took their punishment as Moses ground the calf to dust, mixed it with water and made them drink it. Next time they would think twice before disobeying God.

EXODUS 32

Bishop

SPIES INTO CANAAN

However much the Israelite nation disobeyed God and broke their agreement with him, they were still his people. He continued to guide and care for them because he had chosen them.

God told Moses to construct a sacred tent which they could carry with them. Using the most beautiful and precious materials, together with the skills of the most talented designers and craftsmen among them, they were to make a tabernacle for their God.

When Moses told the people about it, they were enthusiastic. Each family gave some of the treasures they had brought from Egypt: gold, silver, bronze, fine linen, woven wool in blue, purple and red, the best leather, soft sheepskin and precious stones.

There were many skilled workmen in the tribe, but two were outstanding. Their names were Bezalel and Aholiab. These two men were chosen to be in charge of the whole project.

Bezalel and Aholiab gathered together a team of fine craftsmen and set to work. God had outlined the plans to Moses and working to these, the craftsmen built the most splendid tent imaginable. The walls were wooden planks, plated with gold, and the roof was cloth and animal skin. It could be taken down and carried with the Israelites as they travelled.

In the centre of this tent or tabernacle, in its own special inner room, they put the Ark or Covenant Box, made from acacia wood and gold. In it were kept the stone tablets of the law, a jar of manna and Aaron's special staff. This box became special to the Israelites and was carried with great care and ceremony wherever they went. It was a sign that God was always with them.

When the tent was finished, and had been dedicated to God, the same cloud and dazzling light came down over it as had appeared over Mount Sinai. God was with his people.

Aaron and his sons (part of the tribe of Levi) were now dedicated to special office as God's priests. Aaron, as High Priest, was given ceremonial robes to wear, with a breastplate studded with twelve jewels, one for each of the twelve tribes.

One morning, eleven months after they had first come to Sinai, the cloud lifted from above the sacred tent. The Israelites knew it was time to be moving on. They broke camp and began their journey once again. The Covenant Box and furled tent were carried in a place of honour at the head of the march.

The journey was not an easy one. It was marked by constant grumblings, and even minor rebellions. Moses' patience was put to the test many times.

At last they came to the borders of Canaan, in sight of their homeland. It seemed a daunting task to conquer and take possession of the territory. The people asked Moses to send spies to report on the land. To reassure them, Moses agreed. Twelve agents set out into Canaan on a spying mission.

Forty days later they returned. Two of the spies, Joshua and Caleb, were optimisitic. They reported that it was rich farming land. They even brought back a bunch of grapes so large and heavy that they had to carry it between them. But the other spies were more concerned with the strength of the people living there. The local tribes were armed and fierce, they reported. There was even some talk of giants! But Moses remained confident that God would help them overcome any opposition. However, rumours began to spread among the people. "The land is dreadful! It doesn't produce enough for the people there already, let alone us. It is full of giants who could crush us like grasshoppers!" The Israelites came very close to rebellion.

As Moses and Aaron stood before them, pleading with the people to see sense, an angry cry went up. "Let's choose another leader," they shouted. "Someone who will take us back to the comforts of Egypt."

The Israelites had become an angry mob. People stooped down to pick up rocks. They were ready to stone their leaders to death.

Just in time, the shining light of God's presence

came down on the tent and the people stopped. God was furious with the Israelites and might well have destroyed the disobedient there and then. Instead, he promised that none of those people involved in the rebellion would ever see the Promised Land.

So began forty years of travel in the desert before God would allow the Israelites to enter their home.

Once more the Israelites moved off into the desert and pitched camp. There was no water to be found and so they turned to Moses again. God told Moses and Aaron to take the staff from the Covenant Box. He directed them to a water-bearing rock and instructed them to speak to the rock. This time it was Moses who disobeyed. Raising the staff above his head he struck the rock twice, as he had done before. Water gushed out, but God was angry with Moses and Aaron. Neither of them, he said, would lead the people into the Promised Land.

Before long Aaron died and his position as High Priest was taken by his son Eleazar. Despite their complaints, Aaron was loved and respected by the people and they mourned his death.

The Israelites continued to be rebellious and to accuse God of failing to look after them. They even complained that they were bored with the manna he sent them every day. Then they were in trouble.

A vast plague of poisonous snakes hit the camp. Many of the Israelites were bitten and died. Others cried out to Moses. "We should never have doubted the Lord! Please ask God to take the snakes away!"

Moses acted quickly. At God's command, he made a snake out of bronze and fixed it on a pole. Holding it up high, he shouted: "Look at the bronze snake and you will be saved."

Miraculously it happened. Those who, only minutes before, had been at death's door, fixed their eyes on the snake and were healed. The snakes left the camp. God had punished his people, but he had not destroyed them.

EXODUS 35 TO 40; NUMBERS 13; 20 TO 21

After forty days they returned from exploring the country and, coming back to Moses and Aaron and the whole community of Israelites at Kadesh in the wilderness of Paran, they made their report, and showed them the fruit of the country. They gave Moses this account: "We made our way into the land to which you sent us. It is flowing with milk and honey, and here is the fruit it grows; but its inhabitants are formidable, and the towns are fortified and very large;"
Numbers 13:25–28

71

Balaam's Donkey

Balaam was sitting in his house reading his scrolls. He was a prophet who lived far away to the east of Canaan in Mesopotamia. He had the power to put curses on people and was feared and respected by kings and tribal leaders. He was usually happy to provide curses or blessings to order, depending on how much he was paid. But he knew that the Israelite's God, Jehovah, was the all-powerful God of the whole world. If God spoke, he must do as he said.

One day important messengers came to see Balaam. They were men from the tribes of Moab and Midian, sent by King Balak the Midianite leader who was worried about the Israelites. The messengers delivered this message from Balak: "The Israelites are threatening to take over the lands. I want you to come and put a curse on them so that we can drive them away." The messengers had plenty of money to pay for Balaam's services.

That night Balaam had a dream in which God told him that Israel was his own chosen nation. Under no circumstances was he to curse them. So next morning Balaam sent the messengers away with a refusal.

But King Balak was not to be put off easily. He sent more important envoys with even more money. Balaam told them that all the money in the world would be no use to him if he disobeyed God.

That night God spoke to him again. He said: "You may go, but you must only say what *I* tell you to." So next morning Balaam saddled his donkey and set off with King Balak's men.

While he was riding along the road, his donkey suddenly lurched off the road into a field. Balaam, angry at his normally placid donkey, beat the animal with his stick. He could not see what the donkey could see. The Angel of the Lord stood barring the road ahead.

As the angel moved, the donkey moved forward again. Then the angel stopped and the donkey pressed into the side of the road to get out of the way, crushing Balaam's foot against the stone wall. The prophet who still could not see the angel was furious with the animal and beat him again.

The angel moved to an even narrower stretch of the road, blocking it completely. Frightened and bewildered, the donkey just gave up and lay down in the road. Balaam set about the poor beast with his stick. Then he heard the donkey speak: "What have I done to deserve this treatment?" Surprised, Balaam shouted back, "You've made a fool out of me, that's what!" Suddenly, Balaam could see the angel. At once he realized that this divine messenger was sent to remind him that God was watching him.

When Balaam and his party arrived, King Balak took him to a hill where he could see the Israelites. All was ready for Balaam to put his curse on the Israelite nation. But Balaam was aware of the God of Israel protecting his people. He knew they must be blessed, not cursed. So summoning up his courage, Balaam made a great ceremonial speech in praise of Israel and their God.

Balak was confused. Was he paying this man good money so that he could bless his enemy and give them an advantage? He took Balaam to another place to try again, but Balaam told the king: "I can only do what God tells me to," and he recited another poem, blessing the Israelites. Balak was losing his patience. He tried a third time, but with no success.

By now Balak was at the end of his tether. This man persisted in doing exactly the opposite of what he was asked. In despair, he ordered Balaam to leave. But Balaam, speaking with the authority God gave him, began to predict the future. He told everyone that one day a great king would come to rule over Israel, someone who would lead them to victory.

Balak saw all his hopes of victory dashed. He sent Balaam home without any payment and returned to his tribe. He knew that there was no sense in fighting the people God had chosen.

NUMBERS 22–24

THE DEATH OF MOSES

Moses was growing old. Although still fit and strong, he knew he did not have long to live. The Israelite nation was at last poised to cross the river Jordan from the plains of Moab and to enter the land they had been promised so many years before. Moses knew he would not enter the land himself, because of his failure to obey God's command when he struck the rock.

On the eve of their entry into Canaan, Moses was instructed to take a census of all the fit and able men over the age of twenty who were eligible for military service. (The tribe of Levi, the priests, were exempt from fighting.) The Israelite army numbered almost six-hundred-and-two thousand men, but there was not one man left alive of those who had mistrusted God when spies were first sent into the land. Only Joshua and Caleb, the two spies who had remained faithful to God, had survived the forty years in the desert.

Because he was going to die, Moses asked God to appoint a man to lead the people. God chose Joshua, Moses' right-hand man. He was a capable commander, who loved and trusted God.

So Moses gathered the people together and said: "I am one-hundred-and-twenty years old and no longer able to be your leader. I will not go with you to the Promised Land, but God will be with you. You will overcome the nations that live there and make the land your own. You need not fear the tribes. Be confident! God our father will not abandon you!"

Then Moses turned to Joshua and declared to the whole nation that he was to be their new leader. Next he called Eleazar, the High Priest who would interpret God's commands for the nation. He would be with Joshua to lead the people. The tribe shouted their approval.

When the ceremony was over, Moses and Joshua went to the sacred tent where the dazzling light and cloud of God's presence hovered. There they heard God's special instructions. Leading the Israelites would not be easy. They would rebel once more when they entered the land and would turn their backs on God yet again. Joshua would need all God's wisdom and strength for the task.

The Lord gave Moses and Joshua a hymn or national anthem for the people. It spoke of how God had chosen the Israelite nation for himself and protected and cared for them in the desert, "Like an eagle, teaching its young to fly."

Finally, Moses set out for Mount Pisgah to meet God for the last time on Earth. Before he went, he spoke for the last time to his people: "God's commands are not empty words," he told them, "they are your very life, the pattern you should live by, always." Then, with a special word of blessing and encouragement for each of the twelve tribes of Israel, and promising great things for the nation, he left them.

At the peak of the mountain, God showed Moses the land he would never reach, stretching out into the distance.

Soon after this last meeting with God, Moses died. The Israelites never saw him again and to this day, no one has ever discovered Moses' grave.

So ended one dramatic period of Israel's history. Despite slavery, ruthless enemies, hardship, disease and rebellion, the nation had survived. It was on the threshold of a new era under a new leader. As the great tribe, with their flocks of sheep, goats and cattle stood ready to cross the river Jordan, their spirits were high. The Promised Land lay ahead.

DEUTERONOMY 31 TO 34

Harry BISHOP

The Walls of Jericho

God said to Moses' assistant Joshua, "Now that Moses is dead, you are to be the Israelites' leader. Take your people across the River Jordan into the land I am giving them. No enemy will defeat you if you are strong and brave, and obey my laws."

Joshua was not so sure. He knew about the people of Canaan, their towns and cities were strongly defended and they were sure to fight hard to keep out the Israelites.

First, Joshua sent two spies to Jericho, a powerful city protected by high walls. The men pretended to be ordinary travellers, and stayed at the house of a woman called Rahab. But news of the spies reached the king of Jericho, and he sent his police to arrest them.

"The king demands that you bring out the two men staying with you, as we know they are spies," they said. Rahab quickly replied: "Yes, two men were with me but they have just left, if you hurry you should catch them."

So the police hurried away. But in fact Rahab had been very clever; she had hidden the men under piles of flax drying on the flat roof of her house.

With the police gone she said to the spies, "I've helped you, so please spare my family's lives when you take Jericho. I know you *will* take it, for everyone here is afraid of your people."

After they promised she helped them escape. The city gates had been shut, but her house was built into the city wall. So when it grew dark she let down a rope from a window and the spies climbed down.

Back in the Israelite camp they told Joshua, "God will give us this land, for its people fear us."

Then Joshua led all the Israelites over the River Jordan and into Canaan. When the people of Jericho saw the great horde of Israelites coming they shut the gates to keep them out.

But God told Joshua, "The city is already as good as yours. March your army around Jericho once a day for six days. Seven priests with trumpets made of ram's horn must walk behind the troops. Behind the priests, you must carry the Ark of the Covenant.

"On the seventh day you must walk seven times around the city with the priests blowing their trumpets. When they blow one long blast, all the people must give a great shout and then the walls will fall down."

So for six days the besieged citizens wondered why the enemy army marched around the city without making any attack.

At dawn on the seventh day the troops circled Jericho seven times. Then the seven priests sounded a long, loud blast on their trumpets. Joshua called out, "Shout! God has given us the city!"

The Israelites let out a yell and the walls just crumbled to dust. At once the army surged in and took the city.

JOSHUA 1 TO 6

So the trumpets were blown, and when the army heard the trumpets sound, they raised a great shout, and the wall collapsed.
Joshua 6:20

GIDEON'S BATTLE

By the time Joshua died his people had won much of Canaan. But dangers soon threatened the Israelites' hard-won homeland. Swarms of nomads called Midianites rode into the country on camels, smashing and stealing crops, and riding off with the Israelites' sheep, cattle and donkeys. For seven years the Israelites seemed helpless to stop these terrible raids.

Then, one day, an angel visited a poor farmer's son called Gideon. The angel said, "Go now – it's up to you to save the people of Israel from the Midianites."

"How can I do that?" asked Gideon. "My family is the poorest of my tribe and I am the least important member of my family."

But the angel said, "God will be on your side."

First, though, Gideon had to show he was worthy to be leader. He did this by smashing an altar belonging to foreign gods. When these gods failed to punish him the Israelites guessed he was sent by their God.

Soon after this the Midianites and their allies launched a massive attack on the Israelites. Thousands gathered to protect their land. But God said to Gideon, "There are too many. If they beat the Midianites the Israelites will think they won without my help. Send home all those who are scared."

So twenty-two thousand went home, which left only ten thousand.

But God said, "That's still too many. Take them to drink at the spring and I'll show you which ones to take into battle."

When Gideon did that God said, "Make one group from those who cup their hands and drink what they scoop up. Make another group from those who kneel down to drink, with their mouths in the water."

No more than three hundred men drank from their hands. All the rest knelt down to drink.

"I shall save you with just these three hundred men," declared God. "Let all the rest go home."

So Gideon did. That night he gave his men trumpets, and burning brands hidden in clay pots. Then they all crept downhill to the camp of the enemy, who hugely outnumbered Gideon's tiny army.

Just after midnight his men blew their trumpets, and smashed their pots so their three hundred burning brands blazed in the night.

At the same time the three hundred men yelled, "For God and for Gideon." The din was terrifying.

Caught by surprise, the sleepy enemy believed a huge force was attacking. In the darkness and confusion they started killing one another by mistake. Then their great army broke up, and its soldiers simply ran off into the night.

Gideon's victory crushed the Midianites for good, and brought his people years of peace.

JUDGES 6 TO 7

All three companies blew their trumpets and smashed their jars; then, grasping the torches in their left hands and the trumpets in their right, they shouted, "A sword for the Lord and for Gideon!" Every man stood where he was, all round the camp, and the whole camp leapt up in a panic and took flight.
Judges 7:20–21

SAMSON AND DELILAH smith

Once again the Israelites faced a powerful enemy. This time it was the Philistines. These seaborne invaders peopled the coast of what is now Israel. In time they pushed inland and began seizing the fertile plains of Canaan, and the hills where most of the Israelites lived.

The Bible says that the Philistines conquered the Israelites and ruled them for forty years.

But one day came hope of a great new Israelite champion. An angel promised an Israelite woman, "You will soon have a son. He will be special to God and his hair must never be cut. He will be able to save you from the Philistines.

When the son was born his parents named him Samson. He grew up to be amazingly strong. Once, a young lion attacked him, but he killed the beast with his bare hands. Samson slaughtered scores of Philistines singlehanded. Once he killed a thousand men using the jaw bone of an ass as a weapon.

But one day Samson fell in love with a Philistine woman called Delilah. When the Philistine rulers found out, they offered Delilah money if she could learn the secret of Samson's strength. Then they would know how to overcome it and seize him.

When she next saw Samson, Delilah said, "Do tell me the secret of your great strength. How could anyone ever overcome it and tie you up?"

Samson joked, "If people tied me with seven new bowstrings I should be as weak as anyone else."

So the Philistine rulers secretly brought her the bowstrings and she tied him up while he slept.

Then she cried, "The Philistines are here to get you, Samson!" But he snapped the bowstrings as if they were brittle strings.

Delilah complained, "You were just teasing. Go on, tell me truly how someone could tie you up."

Samson teased her a second time, saying, "I'd be helpless if you tied me with brand new ropes."

So this time she bound him with ropes while he slept. But when she shouted as before, he snapped the ropes as if they were threads.

Once more he teased her like this. "If you weave my hair into the cloth on your loom," he said, "I shall become as weak as other men." But when Delilah tried that, Samson dragged the loom away easily.

But Delilah nagged him so often, that at last he told her the truth.

"If my hair is cut, I'll be as weak as an ordinary man."

So Delilah lulled him to sleep as he lay with his head on her lap. Then she called in a barber who cut off Samson's hair.

For the last time Delilah shrilled, "The Philistines are here to get you Samson."

Samson woke up. He thought, "I'll just shake myself free again."

Then came a nasty surprise; his muscles just would not work, and he could not move easily.

The Philistines rushed in. They cruelly gouged out his eyes and bound him with chains. Samson could do nothing to stop them. Then they dragged him off to grind grain in prison at the city of Gaza.

JUDGES 13 TO 16:4–21

Afterwards Samson fell in love with a woman named Delilah, who lived by the wadi of Sorek. The lords of the Philistines went up to her and said, "Cajole him and find out what gives him his great strength, and how we can overpower and bind him and render him helpless."
Judges 16:4–5

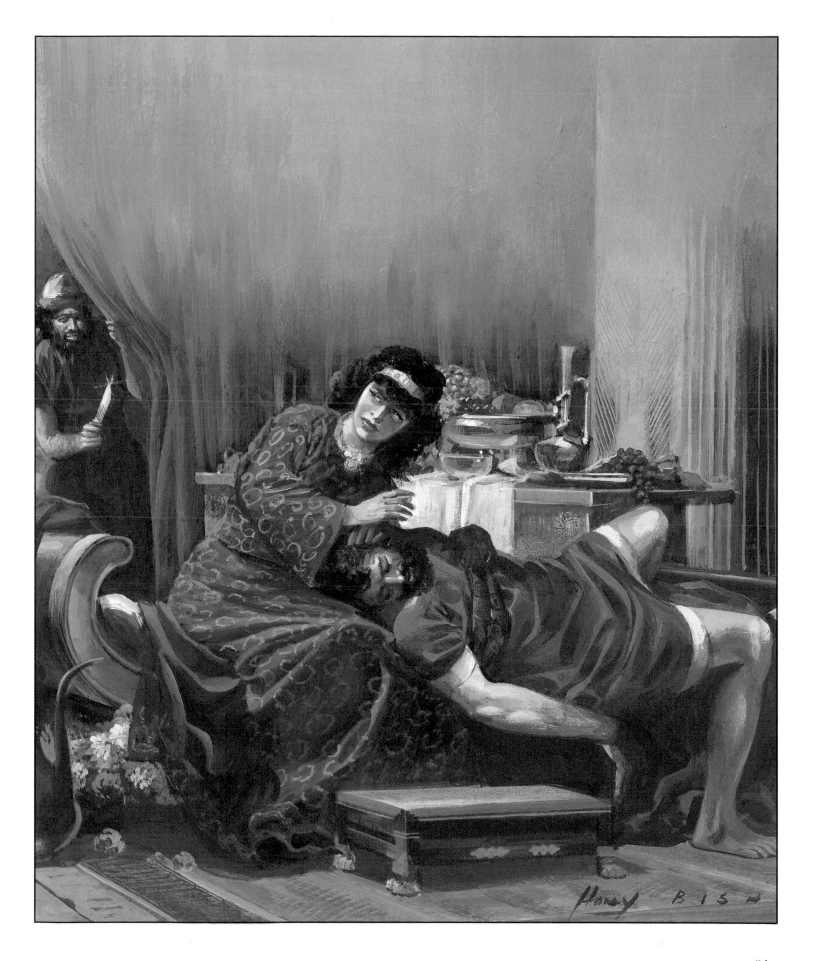

SAMSON IN THE TEMPLE

The Philistines held a temple festival to honour their god Dagon, who was half-man, half-fish, and to praise him for helping them capture Samson. All the people rejoiced and shouted:

"Our god has delivered into our hands Samson our enemy."

When the celebrating crowd was half-drunk, people cried "Fetch Samson! Let's make fun of him!"

So Samson was dragged from jail. The blind Israelite looked weak and harmless. But his hair had begun to grow again and strength was flowing back into his muscles.

The Philistines made him stand between two pillars that held up the temple roof.

Samson said to the boy who guided him, "Put my hands on the pillars so that I can rest against them."

By then the temple was packed with the Philistine leaders, and about three thousand people gazed down from the balconies and poked fun at Samson.

Suddenly Samson cried out, "God, remember me, and strengthen me once more, so I may repay the Philistines at one stroke for blinding my two eyes!"

He pushed against the pillars with both hands, praying, "Let me die with the Philistines."

As the pillars began to give way there came a terrible cracking sound. Then the whole heavy roof thundered down, crushing thousands of people under the rubble.

Samson destroyed more Philistines in one moment at his death than he had killed all through his life.

JUDGES 16:21–31

Samson said to the boy who led him by the hand, "Put me where I can feel the pillars which support the temple, so that I may lean against them."
Judges 16:26

Samson cried to the Lord and said, "Remember me, Lord God, remember me: for this one occasion, God, give me strength, and let me at one stroke be avenged on the Philistines for my two eyes." He put his arms round the two central pillars which supported the temple, his right arm round one and his left round the other and, bracing himself, he said, "Let me die with the Philistines."
Judges 16:28–30

RUTH AND NAOMI

The story of Ruth and Naomi is one of great loyalty and friendship. Naomi and her husband were Israelites who left Israel (as Canaan became known) and settled in a place called Moab. There Naomi's sons and husband died. Naomi was left alone except for her sons' wives, Ruth and Orpah.

Naomi decided to go back to Bethlehem, her home town in Israel. At first both her daughters-in-law insisted on going with her, for they were very fond of Naomi. But Naomi urged, "Go back to your parents' homes in Moab. Maybe you'll find new husbands there."

She kissed them, and all three wept. But Ruth and Orpah said, "No, we'll go with you to your people."

Again Naomi tried to stop them. This time Orpah did turn back, but Ruth refused to leave Naomi. Ruth said, "Where you go, I shall go. Your people shall be my people, and your God my God."

So Ruth bravely kept Naomi company in a land she did not know.

In Bethlehem they were so poor and hungry that Ruth gathered grain spilt by workers reaping a field.

The field belonged to Boaz, a rich relative of Naomi's dead husband. When Boaz learnt who Ruth was, he decided to marry her and help to care for Naomi. So two poor and lonely women found their happiness at last.

RUTH 1 TO 4

SAMUEL AND SAUL

"Samuel! Samuel!" called a voice in the night. The boy Samuel woke up and answered, "Here I am." Then he ran to his master, Eli.

"I didn't call you," muttered the old priest sleepily. "Go back to bed."

But the voice came again – and once more Eli muttered crossly that he had not spoken a word. After a third awakening Eli began to suspect that the voice came from God. So he said more kindly, "Lie down, and if God calls again, say, 'Speak, Lord, for I hear you.'"

Samuel did as the old man suggested. The boy heard the voice again and he answered as Eli had told him. Then the voice described plainly events that had not yet happened. For God had chosen the boy priest to become one of his prophets.

When Samuel grew up he became famous for telling the future. People respected him, and made him a judge. Judges were men chosen by all the Israelite tribes to lead them in times of danger.

Under Samuel his people beat off their old enemies the Philistines. When Samuel grew too old to act as a general, his sons became judges, but they turned out to be greedy and useless.

One day the Israelite elders visited Samuel at his home.

"Things have got bad since you retired and your sons do not rule wisely," they complained. "Give us a king like other nations have."

Samuel felt uneasy about this and prayed to God for advice.

God said, "Let them have what they want. Don't feel the people have turned against you. I'm the one they reject – just as they've so often rejected me in the past. But warn them what being ruled by a king can be like."

So Samuel warned the elders.

"A king will force you to become his soldiers, workers and servants. He'll seize the best of your farmland, a share of your flocks and some of your slaves."

But the people still insisted they wanted a permanent ruler. So Samuel agreed to choose his country's first king.

Soon afterwards, a stranger came to Samuel. He was tall and handsome. His name was Saul, and he was searching for some lost donkeys. Saul hoped that the famous prophet could say where they were.

Samuel could – but he did far more. To Saul's surprise, the old man sat him down at the end of his table, above dozens of more important guests.

The next day, the young man was even more surprised when Samuel made him kneel, and then poured a little olive oil on his head. For this was what priests did when they were crowning a king.

Then Samuel announced, "God has chosen you as king of Israel."

I SAMUEL 3 TO 10:1

Samuel took a flask of oil and poured it over Saul's head; he kissed him and said, "The Lord annoints you prince over his people Israel. You are to rule the people of the Lord and deliver them from the enemies round about."
I Samuel 10:1

SAUL'S SACRIFICE

In his first year as ruler Saul seemed just the kind of strong king the Israelites needed. But old Samuel the prophet still felt uneasy about having made Saul a king. For he knew many kings grew very fond of their power, and sometimes they forgot the laws of religion.

"If you and your king obey God all will be well," Samuel announced to the people. "But God will punish you if you ignore him."

A battle was brewing between the Israelites and Philistines. Samuel, as a prophet-priest, had to offer burnt sacrifices to God, so that God would give the Israelites victory.

But when the old man reached the Israelite army he smelt burnt offerings and saw Saul already stoking the fire. Samuel's eyes blazed fiercely and his face was stern and unfriendly.

"What have you done?" he snapped.

Saul said guiltily, "My men were outnumbered and would have run away when the Philistines attacked. So, as you were late, I thought I should light the fire myself."

"You fool!" thundered Samuel. "By doing this you have disobeyed God. He would have made your descendants kings of Israel for ever, but now you must step down for a man who will truly obey God."

And Samuel warned that God had already chosen Saul's successor.

I SAMUEL 13:1–14

Samuel said to Saul, "You have acted foolishly! You have not kept the command laid on you by the Lord your God; if you had, he would have established your dynasty over Israel for all time."
I Samuel 13:13

DAVID AND GOLIATH

One day an Israelite boy called David took on a Philistine giant single-handed.

David had brought food to his older brothers in the Israelite army. The army was camped on one hill, facing the Philistines on another.

Suddenly a huge man stepped forward from the Philistines' ranks. He wore shining bronze armour and gripped a huge shield and spear.

"Send one man to fight me!" bellowed Goliath the giant. "If he kills me we are your slaves; if I kill him you are ours."

The mere sound of the giant's voice scared the Israelites, and Saul, the Israelite king, knew he had no man strong enough to take on the giant in single combat.

But young David cried out, "Who does this Philistine think he is, defying God's own army?"

David's eldest brother scolded him for speaking so daringly and told him to go and take care of his sheep. But Saul was curious to hear more.

The boy boldly told his king, "Don't worry, I'll fight Goliath."

Saul laughingly asked, "How can a lad like you tackle an experienced soldier like him?"

David answered sturdily, "I've killed lions and bears before now, when they raided my flock; God will protect me."

So Saul doubtfully agreed. He even lent David his armour. But the boy found this too big and heavy, and took it all off. He stepped out armed with no more than a handful of stones and a shepherd's sling.

When Goliath saw a mere child coming to meet him he roared with a loud voice "If you come here I'll feed your flesh to the beasts."

"God will help me do that to you!" David called back. And as he drew closer to the giant, David placed a stone in his sling, whirled it around, and let fly. The stone struck Goliath full on the forehead, knocking him out.

At once David ran up, pulled Goliath's sword

from its sheath and sliced off the giant's head.

When they saw what David had done the Israelites gave a great cheer, and the Philistine army fled in dismay.

I SAMUEL **17**:1–51

The Philistine, preceded by his shield-bearer, came on towards David. He looked David up and down and had nothing but disdain for this lad with his ruddy cheeks and bright eyes.
I Samuel 17:41–42

JONATHAN AND DAVID

Young David the giant-killer became one of King Saul's greatest favourites. He lived in the royal household, and Saul's own son Jonathan was David's best friend. Neither guessed that Jonathan would one day stop Saul from murdering David.

Saul was a difficult, moody man. As David grew up Saul became jealous of David's success as an army leader, and feared he was plotting to seize the throne.

When Saul felt depressed David used to play the king soothing music on a harp-like instrument called a lyre. One day as David quietly strummed away, Saul snatched up a spear and hurled it. David jumped aside – just in time.

David was horrified. He ran away from the royal household and hid. Then he learnt that Saul had sent soldiers to hunt him down.

David went to Jonathan and asked his friend, "Why is your father set on having me killed?"

Jonathan was astonished at such a suggestion. He said, "He's told me nothing of this."

"He wouldn't," said David bitterly. "After all, he knows that you and I are great friends."

"Now listen. Tell Saul I've gone home to Bethlehem. If he says 'That's all right' I'll know it's safe to return. But if he's angry you'll know he really is planning to kill me."

So David stayed hidden while Jonathan went to learn what Saul was planning to do. When he told Saul he had let David go home, Saul was so furious that he almost thrust a spear through his own son.

Next day, as they had arranged, Jonathan took his bow and fired some practice arrows near where David was hiding. Then sent a boy to pick them up.

David knew that if Jonathan called out to the boy, "The arrows are on this side," then he was safe, but if Jonathan shouted, "They're beyond you," he was in danger.

David waited tensely as the first arrows flew. His heart sank as he heard the words, "They're beyond you, look further."

When Jonathan had sent the boy away David crept out. Then the two men sadly said goodbye. But they promised to stay friends for the rest of their lives.

I SAMUEL 18 TO 20

DAVID SPARES SAUL

Once King Saul had made up his mind to kill him, David was forced to live as an outlaw. But there was plenty of sympathy for this good and brave man. More and more people felt that God would prefer David as king. For there was no doubt that Saul was sick in his mind and often mad.

In time, six hundred men had joined David. So Israel was divided, and threatened by civil war.

Because Saul's troops outnumbered David's, David tried to avoid outright battles. He and his men lived off the land and hid in caves, moving on whenever Saul's army approached.

At last, though, Saul almost caught them. Word had come to the king that David was hiding somewhere in a rocky desert where wild goats roamed. So Saul took three thousand troops and went after him.

After a long, fruitless search, Saul went inside a shady cave. He had no idea that farther back in the cave David was hiding with a small band of his men.

Saul had arrived alone and left his troops some way off. When David realized the king was unguarded, he stealthily crept up on Saul.

"Now's your chance," whispered David's supporters. "God's put him into your power."

But instead of killing Saul as his men wanted, David used his sword to secretly slice the hem from Saul's robe.

Even then he felt he had gone too far. He whispered, "I was wrong to do that, for, after all, God did choose Saul to be king."

Saul then left the cave. But while the king was still in earshot of the cave, David stepped out and shouted, "Here's the hem from your robe. I cut it off in the cave. I could easily have killed you too, but I didn't. Doesn't that make you believe I wish you no harm?"

Saul turned, startled. "Is that really you, David?" he called. Then he wept with emotion; for Saul could be soft hearted as well as cruel, as the mood took him. "You are a better man than I, David, for you

repaid my evil with goodness. May God reward you. I know now that one day you will become king of all Israel. Promise me only that when you succeed me you will not kill my descendants."

David promised. Then Saul went home and David returned to his cave. He knew Saul would leave him in peace – until hatred once more poisoned the king's mind.

I SAMUEL 22 TO 24

When David had finished speaking, Saul said, "Is that you, David my son?" and he burst into tears. He said, "The right is on your side, not mine: you have treated me so well; I have treated you so badly. You have made plain today the good you have done me; the Lord put me at your mercy, but you did not kill me."
I Samuel 24:16–18

THE DEATH OF SAUL

Under cover of night three men crept out of King Saul's army camp and knocked at the door of a famous witch. One of the men was the king in disguise.

Saul felt he needed the help of magic, for a huge Philistine army now threatened his weaker, Israelite force. What was worse, his old Israelite enemy David had joined the Philistines and seemed ready to fight against his own people.

Saul believed only the great prophet Samuel could tell him how to win. But Samuel was dead.

As the witch opened her door, Saul said urgently, "I want you to call up the spirit of a dead person so that I can talk to him."

"You're trying to trap me," she snarled. "Everyone knows that the king executes fortune tellers."

Saul promised not to betray her. Then he asked to speak to the spirit of Samuel.

The old man's spirit slowly took shape, and Saul asked him, "What shall I do? The Philistines are attacking us, and God leaves all my prayers for help unanswered."

Samuel's reply was hardly consoling: "If God has left you, why ask me for help? Once, you disobeyed God. Now you must pay the price. Tomorrow your troops will be routed and you and your sons will be killed. Then your rival David will rule in your place."

The terrible words of Samuel's prophecy struck Saul's ears like a deathblow. He fell to the ground, and took some time to recover. At last Saul pulled himself together and trudged back gloomily to his doomed Israelite army.

The battle that followed went as Samuel had foretold. The Philistines smashed through Saul's Israelite army. They slaughtered three of Saul's sons – even David's closest friend, Jonathan. David himself did not fight for the Philistines, although Saul had feared he would. The Philistines sent David away, because they thought he might switch sides and fight for his own people after all.

David's absence did not save Saul. One moment he heard a sound like angry bees buzzing. The next instant, a shower of Philistine arrows was falling and piercing chinks in his armour. Saul staggered, badly wounded; but he refused to be taken alive.

Weak with pain, the king beckoned his armour bearer. "Finish me off with your sword," Saul

gasped, "before these heathens torture me for their pleasure." But the man shrank away at the thought of killing his king.

Then Saul pointed his sword at himself and fell on the tip of the blade. So died the first king of Israel, on what must have seemed its darkest day.

*I SAMUEL **28** TO **31***

He said to his armour-bearer, "Draw your sword and run me through, so that these uncircumcised brutes may not come and taunt me and make sport of me." But the armour-bearer refused; he dared not do it. Thereupon Saul took his own sword and fell on it.
I Samuel 31:4

JOAB KILLS ABNER

The two Israelite soldiers ran panting as if in a race. First came General Abner, commander-in-chief of an army loyal to Saul's son Ishbosheth who now ruled northern Israel. Hard on Abner's heels ran Asahel; Asahel's brother Joab commanded an army loyal to David who ruled southern Israel, known as Judah.

This was no friendly race, but a chase to the death. For Joab's army had just crushed Abner's in a terrible battle, and now Asahel was out to kill Abner.

Abner glanced behind him, calling, "Chase someone else, Asahel. I could never face your brother Joab again if you make me kill you."

But Asahel caught up with Abner, who struck out in self defence with the blunt end of his spear. By bad luck it pierced Asahel and killed him.

When Joab heard what Abner had done he swore his revenge. But Joab could never get near enough

while both generals stayed with their own armies.

Then something quite unexpected happened. Abner quarrelled with his own king, and secretly visited David. Abner offered David the throne of all Israel in exchange for command of the whole Israelite army.

David agreed to this, and Abner set off north to make the arrangements. But he had only just left when Joab returned from a raid. When he learned that David had let his own brother's killer go Joab was furious.

"Why let him go?" Joab demanded. Then Joab secretly sent messengers after Abner to bring him back. As Abner returned, Joab took him aside by the town gate as if he wanted to have a private talk. Then without warning Joab quickly whipped out a dagger and stabbed the defenceless Abner to death.

Joab had avenged his dead brother by an act of treachery that horrified David and spoilt his plans. Even so, in time David did become the king of all Israel.

II SAMUEL 2 TO 3

Must Abner die so base a death?
Your hands were not bound,
your feet not fettered;
you fell as one who falls at the hands
* of a criminal.*
II Samuel 3:33–34

ABSALOM'S REBELLION

Many enemies tried to seize the kingdom of Israel. The most dangerous of all was one of David's own sons, a man called Absalom. This young prince was greatly admired throughout the whole of Israel for his handsome face and figure. His hair hung long and thick about him. He had to cut it every year because he found it so heavy.

Absalom was proud and ambitious, and after quarrelling with David he plotted to seize his father's throne.

News of Absalom's treachery reached David in Jerusalem. Rather than start a war with his own son, David set off into exile with his servants and soldiers.

So Absalom marched his rebellious troops into the capital unopposed. But soon he marched out again – determined to find his father and win victory over him.

David was forced to do battle. But he did not want to harm his son. "Deal gently with Absalom," he told his commanders.

In the struggle that followed, Absalom's side was defeated. Absalom tried to escape through a forest, but his mule galloped under an oak tree and his long hair caught in the branches. One of David's men found him hanging there helplessly, and told Joab.

"Why didn't you kill him?" David's commander demanded angrily.

"Because the king said that we should protect him," came the reply.

But to Joab, Absalom was a traitor. He took three spears, rode up to the terrified enemy leader, and stabbed him to death as he hung.

II SAMUEL 14:25–33 TO 18:1–17

Some of David's men caught sight of Absalom; he was riding his mule and, as it passed beneath a large oak, his head was caught in its boughs; he was left in mid-air, while the mule went on from under him.
II Samuel 18:9

SOLOMON THE WISE

Israel had no king so wise or so powerful as David's son Solomon. He was young and inexperienced when he came to the throne. But God visited him in a dream and asked what help he needed.

Solomon replied, "An understanding mind that will help me rule well, and know right from wrong."

God was pleased with this sensible answer. "You shall be the world's wisest man," he promised. "Also, no other king will be so rich or famous as you for as long as you live."

Solomon soon had a chance to show his wisdom, for two angry women asked him to settle a dispute.

"Your Majesty," explained one, "each of us had a baby, but hers died. Then she stole mine while I was asleep in the same house."

"No! The living baby is mine – yours is the dead one!" interrupted the second woman.

"That's not true – it's the other way around!" shouted the first.

While they quarrelled noisily, Solomon quietly

made up his mind how he would settle the matter.

Then he said, "Bring a sword. Cut the live baby in half, and give each woman one of the halves."

The idea of seeing her baby killed was too much for the true mother. She cried, "Let the other woman have him, my lord. Don't kill the child."

But the woman who had stolen the child lacked a true mother's feelings. "Divide it!" she urged.

The king gave his decision: "Give the baby to the first woman, for she is its mother."

News of Solomon's judgement spread all over Israel and people were much impressed by his wisdom.

Under Solomon, Israel built up a wealthy trading empire. The country grew rich, partly by charging taxes to merchants who had to cross Israel on their journeys between what are now Egypt, Iraq and Turkey. Solomon's ships sailed away on long expeditions. They came back brimming with amazing treasures such as apes, peacocks and ivory. His camel caravans plodded deep into the Arabian deserts to fetch rare and expensive spices. Cloth, horses and mules were among the rich gifts brought in each year from admiring kings.

No wonder Solomon could afford to sit on a gold and ivory throne, eating and drinking from cups and plates of pure gold. No wonder he owned hundreds of chariots and thousands of horses. The king could afford to live in a splendid palace and keep hundreds of wives.

Marrying foreign princesses was one clever way in which Solomon made friends with their fathers – the kings of neighbouring lands.

I KINGS 3 TO 4

SOLOMON'S TEMPLE

For almost five hundred years the Ark of the Covenant – the Israelites' holiest object which contained God's laws – had travelled wherever the Israelites went. Now Solomon built a splendid temple at Jerusalem to hold it.

The far-seeing king spared neither time nor expense. He wanted to make the temple one of the world's finest buidings. What Israel could not supply in fine timber or skills, Solomon bought from abroad.

First he sent a message to his friend King Hiram of Tyre, saying, "Please send foresters to cut cedar wood from the mountains of Lebanon. I'll pay whatever wages you ask."

Hiram replied, "You can have cedar, and cypress too. My men will drag the logs down to the sea, then float them along to your shore. You can pay for the wood with food supplies for my household."

So that is what happened.

The scale of the building work was vast. Solomon called up tens of thousands of workers from all over Israel. Some cut and trimmed wood. Others quarried and shaped stone blocks for foundations. There were miners and metalsmiths too.

At last, after seven long years, the magnificent temple was finished. Two bronze pillars as tall as a house guarded its great doors. These were of carved olive wood covered with thin sheets of beaten gold. Inside, carved cedar-wood panels lined the stone walls.

The Ark of the Covenant stood in an inner room. Two immense golden angels guarded the Ark, and beaten gold gleamed from the ceiling and walls. Even the furniture and tools in the temple were gold.

Solomon held a great celebration to open the temple. It went on for a fortnight, and people came from all over Israel to see the priests sacrifice sheep, goats and cattle. God was well pleased with Solomon for all he had achieved.

I KINGS 5 TO 8

Solomon overlaid the inside of the house with red gold and drew a veil with golden chains across in front of the inner shrine. The whole house he overlaid with gold until it was all covered;
I Kings 6:21–22

THE QUEEN OF SHEBA

Everyone wanted to learn about Solomon's wisdom and wealth – even the Queen of Sheba who lived in far-off southern Arabia. Maybe she felt a little jealous of Solomon, for she too was rich and intelligent.

One day the queen piled gifts of gold, jewels and spices on an army of camels. Then she set off north to visit Jerusalem.

Solomon had never received such valuable presents, or had his brains tested by such tricky

questions as those the queen asked him.

Yet to the Queen of Sheba's surprise he more than matched her gifts with ones of his own, and solved all the problems she set him.

The queen admired his beautiful palace tended by splendidly uniformed servants. Then she said, "At first I couldn't believe what I had heard about your great wisdom and wealth, but now I see that it's true after all."

I KINGS 10

The queen of Sheba heard of Solomon's fame and came to test him with enigmatic questions. She arrived in Jerusalem with a very large retinue, camels laden with spices, gold in vast quantity, and precious stones.
I Kings 10:1–2

Elijah said to Elisha, "Stay here: for the Lord has sent me to Bethel." Elisha replied, "As the Lord lives, your life upon it, I shall not leave you."
II Kings 2:2

ELIJAH AND ELISHA

Elijah the prophet grew old and knew he must soon die. But he did not want to worry his friend Elisha. So Elijah just said, "Wait here while I go on a journey."

But Elisha replied, "I'll go wherever you go." For Elisha had guessed what was going to happen.

Each time they came to a town, Elijah asked Elisha to wait, and each time he refused. At last they stood by the river Jordan, watched by fifty men who admired Elijah's work as God's messenger.

"Stay here while I go across on God's business," Elijah ordered. But Elisha would not be left behind.

As the young men watched with amazement, Elijah struck the river with his rolled cloak and the water parted. Then the two prophets walked across on dry land.

At the far side, Elijah knew his end was near. He sadly asked, "What is your last wish before I am taken away from you?"

Elisha answered, "To be twice as powerful a prophet as you."

"Your wish will be granted if you see me go," came the answer. Suddenly a dazzling glow shone between them and became fiery horses pulling a fiery chariot.

Elisha gasped with astonishment, for Elijah seemed to be swept up with the chariot as it soared into the sky and then vanished.

Only Elijah's cloak was left to show where the prophet had stood. Elisha nervously picked it up and turned back to the river. He struck it with the cloak as Elijah had done. Again the water parted. The watchers knew that although Elijah was dead, God's power lived on in Elisha.

II KINGS 2:1–15

JOSIAH AND THE BOOK OF THE LAW

"Your Majesty, see what the high priest has just found in the temple!" His secretary carefully handed King Josiah of Judah some old yellow scrolls. (In those days people wrote on sheets made from papyrus reeds, and they rolled up each sheet for safekeeping.)

Josiah unrolled one scroll gingerly, for it was brittle with age. As he read, the king turned pale with terror. For the scroll set out some of God's laws that had long been forgotten – and worse than that, they had been most dreadfully disobeyed.

Kings like Josiah's own father and grandfather had been largely to blame. No one could say that grandfather Manasseh followed God's laws. He had practised black magic. In God's own temple at Jerusalem he had built altars to heathen gods like the sun, moon and stars. He had even had his own son burnt to death as a gift for a heathen god.

At least Josiah himself had behaved better. He had repaired the temple, for instance. But even he had unknowingly broken some laws.

Josiah knew God punished disobedience severely. He worried that he might be already preparing a storm, an earthquake or some other frightful disaster.

The king called his advisers together. He said, "Ask God what we should do. For we and our ancestors have not behaved as this book says we ought."

So the high priest, the king's secretary and other important officials set off to find Huldah, a prophetess well known as someone God used as a messenger.

They came back with very bad news of God's plans: "I shall destroy Jerusalem and make the land desolate. But because you are sorry for what has happened, Josiah, I shall wait until you are dead."

Josiah at once called a great meeting. Priests, prophets, rich men and poor – thousands swarmed into Jerusalem. Soon a vast crowd packed the space in front of the temple. A great murmuring arose as the mystified citizens asked one another what was going to happen.

Silence fell as the king appeared by the temple door. Josiah unrolled the first scroll. Then, one by one, he read out God's laws in a clear voice for all to hear.

Afterwards the king made the people join him in promising to obey all God's commands from then on.

Josiah was as good as his word. He emptied the temple of all signs of heathen worship. He smashed heathen altars and idols. He even had heathen priests put to death. The people of Judah had never been so faithful to God, as when Josiah was king.

II KINGS 22 TO 23:1–25

No king before him had turned to the Lord as he did, with all his heart and soul and strength, following the whole law of Moses; noa did any king like him appear again.
II Kings 23:25

THE SORROWS OF JOB

The story of Job is one of great suffering. Job had to trust God no matter what happened – and the things that happened to Job were really terrible.

Job had always been a good, God-fearing man, and God rewarded him by making him rich. He owned thousands of camels and sheep, and hundreds of donkeys and cows. Scores of servants scurried about in his service. Job spent his wealth generously – he often gave big family parties.

God felt so proud of Job's goodness that he even told Satan about it. The evil angel was unimpressed.

"Job only worships you because you made him rich," he sneered. "Just let me make him poor, and *then* see what he calls you."

God agreed, so sure did he feel that Job would stay faithful. So Satan flew off and quickly started making Job's life a misery.

The first sign of things going badly wrong was when an exhausted messenger ran up to Job's house. "The Sabaeans have stolen your cattle and donkeys," he gasped. "They've killed all the herdsmen as well. I'm the only one who escaped."

Before he had finished, another man burst in, shouting, "Lightning has struck your sheep and shepherds, and slaughtered the lot."

A third messenger arrived to say all Job's camels had been stolen. Then came the fourth and heaviest blow of all, the roof of a house had collapsed, killing all of Job's sons and daughters.

One moment Job had been a rich, happy, family man. Now he was suddenly poor, childless and half crazed with grief. Yet instead of blaming God, he said "God gave me all I had, so it was his to take away."

Satan could hardly believe his ears. But he refused to give up. He struck Job again. This time horribly painful boils broke out all over Job's body.

Job's wife felt bitterly angry. "Why don't you curse God?" she moaned. "It's all his fault."

Job felt so ill he wished he had never been born. Yet he only said, "We can't expect God to hand out pleasant things all the time."

Three friends who came to offer their sympathy proved even less help than Job's wife. They said things like, "Stop moaning! *You* must be to blame if God is punishing you. Good people don't suffer like this."

Job knew this was untrue. But each time he tried saying so his friends refused to believe him.

At last God brought the miseries to an end. He explained to Job that no man can always understand why suffering happens. Then God again gave Job health, wealth and children. His patience had been rewarded.

JOB 1 TO 42

"Naked I came from the womb,
naked I shall return whence I came.
The Lord gives and the Lord takes away;
blessed be the name of the Lord."
Job 1:21

113

JEREMIAH'S WARNINGS

"If we stay shut up here we'll all be killed, or die of disease or hunger," warned Jeremiah. King Zedekiah of Judah could not disagree with God's prophet, for he knew that a huge Babylonian army surrounded Jerusalem. Before long the city would have to stop fighting.

Yet Zedekiah stubbornly refused to admit he was beaten. And he lost patience with anyone who preached defeat. Zedekiah was especially annoyed with Jeremiah; the prophet seldom opened his mouth without telling of some disaster ahead.

So Zedekiah grew very angry indeed when Jeremiah went on to say, "If you surrender, God will make sure that our lives are spared."

What Jeremiah said was just commonsense, but to Zedekiah it sounded like treason.

Jerusalem's city officials shared this suspicion, so the king did not care when they had Jeremiah flogged and thrown in a dungeon.

Jeremiah lay there in the dark, half starved, for several days. Then Zedekiah had him brought out.

"Any message from God?" he asked.

"Yes," replied Jeremiah. "The Babylonians will defeat you." Then Jeremiah asked, "Why have you put me in prison? I have never done anyone any harm. Don't send me back there – I'll die."

So Zedekiah relented a little. Instead of the dungeon, Jeremiah found himself in the palace prison – a more comfortable jail. And while there was bread to spare he got a small loaf each day.

But things quickly got worse for Jeremiah when word went around that he still expected defeat. Men complained to the king. "His treacherous prophecies will make our troops lose heart," they said. "He must die!"

So Zedekiah let them drag Jeremiah from his cell and put him into a well. It was empty, but Jeremiah found himself sinking into a soft, smelly layer of mud in the bottom. There he was left without food.

Jeremiah would surely have died but for a kind African palace official named Ebed-melech. When he learnt what had happened, he pleaded with Zedekiah to have Jeremiah brought up. Once more the king changed his mind and relented.

Soon Jeremiah heard voices above. Then something came snaking down into the well. Men were lowering old, soft rags tied to ropes.

"Tie the rags under your armpits," shouted Ebed-melech. "They'll stop the ropes chafing your skin."

Jeremiah obeyed, and they hauled him up. Then it was back to jail. Jeremiah was still in prison when the Babylonians swarmed into the city, just as he had said they would.

JEREMIAH 37 TO 38

"These are the words of the Lord: Whoever remains in this city will die by sword, famine, or pestilence, but whoever surrenders to the Chaldaeans will survive,"
Jeremiah 38:2

THE VALLEY OF BONES

Among the thousands of captives who trudged the dusty roads from Judah to Babylon was a tough, clear-thinking man – the prophet Ezekiel. Ezekiel was determined that whatever happened, his people should never forget their God or homeland.

This wasn't easy. Life became pleasant in Babylon for many Jews, as the people of Judah were now called. It was true they had foreign masters, but Babylon was rich, and anyone clever or skilled had a chance to find a good job. Jews became successful businessmen, lawyers and manufacturers – some even became courtiers.

They also found much to admire, for Babylon was a splendid city to live in. Fine villas and palaces lined the banks of the great Euphrates River. There were broad avenues, tall city walls, and magnificent buildings with immense metal gates. Plants of all kinds grew in the great hanging gardens – one of the seven wonders of the world.

Soaring above all this was a high tower, a square-sided, man-made mountain of brick, rising by giant steps – each step painted a different colour. On top stood a room said to be visited by a god.

Ezekiel warned the Jews against worshipping all such foreign gods. But he did much more than that. He offered Jews hope for the future. Perhaps best of all, he promised that one day God would give them back their lost homeland under the rule of a just king.

This was not wishful thinking. In a strange waking dream Ezekiel had seen what was going to happen. This is how he explained it.

"I seemed to be in a valley full of the scattered bones of human skeletons. The Spirit of God took me among them, and asked me:

'Can these dead bones ever come alive again?'

"I replied, 'Only you can answer that question, Lord.'

"Then the Spirit told me to say to the bones, 'Dry bones, God says he will clothe you with muscles and skin, and breathe life back into your bodies.' So I repeated these words.

"When I stopped speaking I heard a strange rattling. Suddenly the scattered bones were coming together to make whole skeletons. And this was only the beginning. Sinews and flesh and skin all joined the bones and made people – but only dead ones."

"Then God's spirit said, 'Call up the winds and breathe life into these dead bodies.'

"So I did, and the bodies began breathing. Then they stood up, and suddenly the valley was filled by a vast living crowd."

In this way Ezekiel told the Jews that their own dead kingdom would live again. And he was right.

EZEKIEL 37

DANIEL IN THE LIONS' DEN

The jailers seized Daniel and threw him into a den of hungry lions. In moments their teeth must surely be crunching his bones. Yet only hours before Daniel had been one of the most powerful men in the entire Persian Empire.

What had happened was this. Daniel had been living in Babylon when the Persians invaded and made it part of the largest empire the world had yet seen. It was too big for the emperor, Darius, to run alone. So he ruled through one hundred and twenty governors – one for each of his empire's provinces. In charge of these governors he placed three presidents. The wisest was Daniel – so wise that Darius planned to put Daniel in charge of the rest. This made the others jealous, for Daniel was a Jew – an outsider in the Persian Empire.

Daniel's enemies plotted to get rid of him. It proved difficult; he was so honest and loyal they could find no reason for persuading Darius to sack him. Then they remembered that Daniel was very religious, and said his prayers to the Jewish God – a different God from theirs.

One day some of Daniel's enemies visited the emperor and suggested a new law to test his subjects' loyalty. "Your Majesty," they fawned, "we propose that any person asking a favour of anyone but yourself in the next thirty days shall be thrown to the lions in your zoo."

The unsuspecting Darius agreed. They then quickly came back to say Daniel was ignoring the new law by praying to God and asking him favours.

Darius was furious at having been tricked into killing his favourite subject. He sadly ordered Daniel's arrest, and walked with him to the mouth of the lions' den to say goodbye.

The emperor's voice broke with grief when he said to Daniel, "May your God save you." Darius felt sure he was seeing Daniel for the last time as the jailers pushed him inside the den.

Darius felt so wretched with worry that night, he could hardly sleep. Early next morning he ran to the lions' den. He knew it was hopeless, Daniel must be dead. Yet something made him call out, "Daniel, did your God save you?"

Darius gave a start of surprise as a voice from inside the den called back, "God kept me safe – the lions didn't touch me."

The emperor was overjoyed. He had Daniel brought out at once, and found him not even scratched. Then Darius threw Daniel's accusers to the lions. This time, no one came out alive.

DANIEL 6

Then the king gave the order for Daniel to be brought and thrown into the lion-pit, but he said to Daniel, "Your God whom you serve at all times, may he save you."
Daniel 6:16

JONAH AND THE GREAT FISH

No prophet had a more terrifying adventure than Jonah – a man swallowed alive by a huge fish.

It was his own fault, of course; he had disobeyed God's orders.

God had told Jonah, "Go to the city of Nineveh in Assyria, and tell its wicked people I will destroy them."

But Jonah did not like the idea of trudging all the way to Assyria only to make its people hate him. So he ran away in the opposite direction. He bought a ticket for a boat sailing to Spain, then he climbed into the hold and fell asleep.

God, however, was not to be cheated. Soon the sky darkened, a fierce gale whipped up the waves, and the ship reared and plunged like a wild beast. Passengers and seamen screamed with fear. Sailors threw cargo overboard to lighten the vessel, and the captain made everyone pray to their gods, to please whichever angry god had sent the hurricane. But the storm raged on.

Then the captain found Jonah, still fast asleep. "Wake up!" he bellowed. "Up on deck and pray to your God to save us."

The sailors thought someone on board was bringing bad luck on the voyage. They cast lots to find out who it was, and Jonah was singled out. The sailors were frightened and started to question Jonah.

"It's all my fault for disobeying my God – the only

real God," Jonah confessed. "The one way to stop the storm is to throw me overboard."

Desperate with fear, the sailors agreed, and hurled Jonah into the raging sea. At once it calmed down.

As the waves closed over his head Jonah knew he was finished.

Suddenly came a loud gulping sound and Jonah felt himself sucked into a great, dark cave – a cave that rumbled and moved. He was inside the jaws of a huge fish.

For three days and nights poor Jonah crouched or squelched around in the darkness. Then he prayed: "If you save me God, I'll do anything you want."

Jonah's prayer was answered. He soon heard sand grating under the fish's belly. Then light dazzled his eyes as the monster's jaws gaped wide. The beast gave a giant cough, and Jonah found himself shot from the fish's mouth on to dry land.

You can be sure that Jonah never again tried escaping from God.

JONAH 1 TO 4

The Lord ordained that a great fish should swallow Jonah, and he remained in its belly for three days and three nights."
Jonah 1:17

The Prodigal Son, page 174

122

THE NEW TESTAMENT

The New Testament is the story of Jesus written by people who, it is believed, knew him or had first-hand accounts of his words and deeds.

Although the books were not written for at least thirty years after Jesus' life, they are as immediate as, say, the memoirs of people writing today about their experiences during the Second World War. People who have witnessed important events can recall them with amazing clarity for many, many years.

So it was with the Gospel writers. They witnessed events which were so remarkable that memories of them were likely to be printed clearly on their minds, never to be forgotten.

We know the events were remarkable, not just from the stories themselves, but from the way people reacted to them. The message of Jesus touched people so profoundly that, despite persecution, they insisted on spreading the good news.

Even the Christian persecutor, Saul, was converted and dedicated his life to travelling and preaching. Later generations, who came to know him as Saint Paul, have relied on his letters to the early Christians to help them learn more about Jesus.

The Gospel stories are set in the Middle East, largely in the countries known today as Jordan, Syria and Israel. At the time, nearly 2000 years ago, the people of the region were living under Roman rule. Some of them joined forces with the Romans, others fought against them and were seen by the authorities as the terrorists of their day. It is into this political turmoil that Jesus was born and against this background that his message was heard.

Some Jewish people thought Jesus was God's promised leader come to overthrow the Romans, but Jesus' message was one of peace not violence.

Christians say he was more than the promised leader, or Messiah; that he was God himself. And, they say, God, the all powerful creator did not come to lead an armed struggle, but was born in poverty and died the death of a humiliated criminal. And the reason? So that the sins of everyone could be forgiven through his death and resurrection.

Exactly how God became a man is something debated endlessly by scholars. What is undeniable is that the Bible stories of the New Testament have inspired generations of Christians to follow Jesus Christ, to live by his teachings and to find God through him.

Some of the stories from the Gospels take the form of simple, understandable advice on how to live a good life. The advice is often difficult to live up to, but has never been bettered. Other stories are full of deep meaning and need to be read many times for the complete message to become clear.

That is not to say the reader has to be clever to understand Christ's message. Faith is a direct experience, a strong inner conviction that what is being said is true. Jesus first preached to men and women with few if any academic achievements. His disciples, the men who were to carry on with his work of preaching and healing, were ordinary folk and some of them probably could barely read or write.

And the Gospel stories are certainly not for adults only. Jesus made a point of rebuking his disciples when they tried to stop the children from talking to him. He said that his message had to be understood with the trust and wonder of childhood and not the sophisticated maturity of adulthood.

The Church remembers the things that happened to Jesus event by event through the year. His ministry, which lasted three years, is squeezed into just twelve months. So it is that his birth is celebrated every Christmas. A little later Lent is observed and Jesus's forty-day fast in the wilderness is recalled. And in Holy Week the stories of Christ's trial and execution are told, followed on Easter Sunday by the joy of his raising from the dead.

Every time the familiar stories are told, Christians find in them new hope and meaning.

TED HARRISON

A SON FOR ZECHARIAH

Today was the most important day in Zechariah's life. As a member of the tribe of Levi, he was one of the priests of the Temple at Jerusalem. He could expect to offer incense in the Holy Place only once in his lifetime, and at last he had been chosen.

Zechariah was a good man, respected and loved by all those who knew him. He was growing old, and while he was more than content in his work, he had suffered one great disappointment. All their married lives he and his wife Elizabeth had wanted a child. Even though they had prayed constantly for children, the years had passed and they eventually realized that it was too late. They could not expect an answer to their prayers now. Even so, Zechariah and his wife had never lost their love for God. Their faith remained unshaken.

Now it was evening. As Zechariah stepped into the Holy Place, in the very centre of the Temple, a large crowd of worshippers gathered outside. He expected to offer up the incense and then to return to lead the people in their prayers. Suddenly he stopped. Something or someone was standing beside the altar.

The old man stood still in terror. He knew that it was an angel, a messenger from heaven.

The angel spoke. "Do not be afraid Zechariah! God has heard your prayers and you will have a son. You must call him John. He will grow up to be a great prophet and will prepare the nation for the coming of the Messiah."

Zechariah could not believe his ears. "But it's not possible," he said. "We're too old to have children."

The angel seemed to blaze with power. "I am Gabriel, God's messenger," he said. "I have brought this good news, yet you refuse to believe it. Because of your disbelief, you will be struck dumb until the day my promise comes true." Zechariah sank to his knees. When he finally looked up, he was alone.

Outside the Temple sanctuary, people were getting restless. Their priest had been gone far longer than usual. Suddenly, the doors opened and Zechariah came out. He looked dazed and he stumbled slightly. He held up his hands for silence, but he did not speak. Instead, he made the sign of the blessing over them and then motioned them to leave. Slowly, the crowd went away, buzzing with curiosity.

Zechariah finished the remainder of his week's Temple service in Jerusalem. Then he returned home wondering how he was going to explain it all to his wife Elizabeth.

Neither of them could really believe what had happened. During the following weeks they both waited excitedly. Before long Elizabeth knew that she was indeed expecting a baby. Their prayers had been answered.

For the first five months of her pregnancy, Elizabeth stayed indoors, sharing her wonderful secret with only close friends and relatives. This was to be no ordinary baby and Elizabeth needed time to prepare herself. Now that the angel's words had begun to come true, there could be no doubt that the Messiah would come soon.

LUKE 1:5–25

There appeared to him an angel of the Lord, standing on the right of the altar of incense. At this sight, Zechariah was startled and overcome by fear. But the angel said to him, "Do not be afraid, Zechariah; your prayer has been heard: your wife Elizabeth will bear you a son, and you are to name him John. His birth will fill you with joy and delight, and will bring gladness to many;"
Luke 1:11–14

THE ANNUNCIATION

When Elizabeth was six months pregnant, in the Galilean town of Nazareth, another strange event occurred. Gabriel, God's messenger, appeared again, this time to a girl called Mary who was a relative of Elizabeth.

Mary's parents had just arranged for her marriage to a young man called Joseph. He and his family were local carpenters and builders. The engagement period would be about a year before the couple could be married.

While Mary was sitting alone one day, she was suddenly aware of a strange being standing in front of her. It was the angel Gabriel. "I bring you greetings, Mary!" he said. "The Lord is with you and has greatly blessed you."

Mary was amazed. She could not think what he could mean. "Do not be afraid, Mary," the angel said. "God has chosen you to be the mother of his son. You will call him Jesus. He will be a king, just as his ancestor David was, and his reign will never end."

"But I am not married yet," Mary said. "God's Holy Spirit will begin the life that will be your baby," the angel replied. "For this reason the child will be set apart for God. He will be called the Son of God.

"And I bring you more news," Gabriel continued. "A member of your family, Elizabeth, is also to have a son. Although it was thought impossible, she is now six months pregnant. There is nothing God cannot do."

Mary gazed at God's messenger. She could not really understand what he was saying, but she knew that he came from God. "I know I belong to God," she said. "I am ready to do whatever he wants."

When Mary was alone again, she went over in her mind what the angel had said. She realized that God was going to send the Saviour they had been waiting for. And he had chosen her to be his mother.

She believed what the angel had said, but would anyone else?

LUKE 1:26–38

Gabriel's Message to Mary

*"Do not be afraid Mary
for God has been gracious to you;
you will conceive and give birth to a son,
and you are to give him the name Jesus.*

*He will be great, and will be called
   Son of the Most High.
The Lord God will give him
   the throne of his ancestor David,
and he will be king over Israel for ever;
his reign shall never end.*

*The Holy Spirit will come upon you,
and the power of the Most High
   will overshadow you;
for that reason the holy child to be born
   will be called Son of God."*
Luke 1:30–33, 35

Mary Visits Elizabeth

It had been much easier for Mary to believe what the angel had told her than to try to tell her family about it. They were good people, who loved and served the God of Israel. Like everyone else they were eagerly awaiting the Messiah. But it was very hard to believe that he had been promised, by an angel, to their own daughter Mary.

Mary said no more. She would wait and see. It had been so difficult to convince her parents, that she began to wonder whether it had all been a dream.

It was especially hard for Mary to tell Joseph. He was a good person, who served God faithfully. If Mary was going to have a baby, it would make things very difficult for the engaged couple. Normally it would mean the end of the engagement.

Mary's thoughts dwelt on the one clear piece of information the angel had brought. Elizabeth was also expecting a baby. If this was true, then everything was true. Mary longed to go and see Elizabeth; she realized she had to go.

It was not easy for Mary to persuade her family to let her go. But they were also anxious for news of Elizabeth and Zechariah. And if Mary was away, it would help to stop the rumours that had already begun to spread around Nazareth.

Mary found a place with a caravan of travellers making the long journey to Elizabeth's home in the hills outside Jerusalem. No one travelled that dangerous route alone.

The journey took five days. On the evening of the fifth day, the small group arrived in the village, hot, dusty and tired. Mary made her way to Zechariah's house. She was more nervous than ever at what she would find. She need not have worried.

As soon as she heard Mary at the door, Elizabeth's baby gave a jump, as if he knew what was happening. Elizabeth knew then that Mary would be the mother of the Messiah, the one her own son must prepare for. Her mind filled with beautiful thoughts and she exclaimed "Mary, you are blessed among women.

Your child will be blessed also. And blessed am I that the mother of the one who will be Lord, should come here to visit me."

Mary also felt the power of God's Spirit when she

saw Elizabeth. Words she had known from childhood, passages from the sacred scriptures, sprang to her lips: "My heart praises the Lord, my soul is glad because of God my saviour. For he has remembered me, his lowly servant! And from now on all people will call me blessed, because of the great things the mighty God has done for me. His name is Holy."

Mary stayed with Elizabeth during the last three months of her pregnancy to give her encouragement and support as the day of the birth drew near.

Mary was happy to be with Elizabeth. The signs of her own pregnancy were beginning to show. It was not easy for her to get used to the amazing idea that she was soon to be a mother.

Mary stayed with Elizabeth for several months. Then she joined a group of travellers heading for Galilee and home.

LUKE 1:39–56

And when Elizabeth heard Mary's greeting, the baby stirred in her womb.
Luke 1:41

129

THE BIRTH OF
JOHN THE BAPTIST

The time for the birth of Zechariah and Elizabeth's baby was drawing near. There was much excitement among her family and friends. Zechariah was still unable to speak since the angel had spoken to him in the Temple. He had to make signs or write things down if he wanted to communicate.

One day, Elizabeth began to feel birth pains that meant the baby was about to be born. A neighbour had come in to help Elizabeth and everything was ready for the event. A few hours later, the baby was born. It was a boy. Everyone was tremendously happy.

It was a special joy for Elizabeth to hold her tiny son, after so many years of waiting. He had been born, just as the angel had promised. Zechariah, not able to say anything, beamed with pleasure.

When the baby was eight days old, all Zechariah's friends and relations arrived for the ceremony of circumcision. They made a very happy party. Zechariah greeted all the guests and there were hugs and kisses, laughter and tears of joy, as everyone heaped congratulations on the old couple.

No one gave the slightest thought about the boy's name. He would be called Zechariah. It was usual for the first son to be called after his father and grandfather. As people admired the baby and tickled him under the chin, they called him by what they thought was his name, Zechariah. Imagine their shock when Elizabeth said seriously, "No, his name is John."

"But you don't have one single relative called John," they said. For a moment the celebration and laughter died down. They looked at Zechariah. He was head of the household and he had the final say. They asked him what the baby boy's name was to be.

Very deliberately Zechariah signed for them to bring him something to write with. A writing tablet was found. It was a tense moment as Zechariah wrote: "His name is John". Everyone gasped. "John!" – the name meant 'God is kind'.

The once happy family party was puzzled and confused, but this turned quickly to wonder as Zechariah opened his mouth and spoke. It was the first time he had uttered a word for almost a year. He leapt to his feet and began to praise God in a strong voice. The people in the house were a little afraid. It was obvious that Zechariah was speaking with a power given to him by God.

He lifted his arms and cried: "Let us praise the Lord, God of Israel. For he has come to help his people and set them free." He told them that God was about to raise up someone mighty, the one Israel's holy men had always promised would come. This person would be more than a man. He would save the people of Israel from their enemies, and have the power to forgive their sins.

Then, turning to his baby son John, he said: "You, my child will be called a prophet of the Most High God." He told John that God had chosen him to spend his life telling others about the person God would send. He was to tell them that the Messiah was coming very soon. John would be God's messenger to his countrymen, the greatest honour anyone could have.

When Zechariah had finished speaking his friends and relations realized that they had heard an important prophecy. What had started out as a party, had turned into an important occasion.

As the guests left the house, they were full of excitement and wonder at everything that had happened. Of course they told their friends about it and the news spread throughout the district. The people thought about Zechariah's words and wondered what kind of child John would be.

As John grew up, it became obvious that there was something special about him. He grew quickly and was a good pupil at the synagogue school. He learnt all he could from the scriptures and from his father.

Zechariah and Elizabeth told John, as fully as they could, the special events which marked his birth.

They taught him the prophecy that had been given to Zechariah at his circumcision and naming. And they discussed the work God had called him to do in preparing for the Messiah, Mary's son.

The young John spent a lot of his time alone, going on long walks into the surrounding hill country. People wondered what he would do with his life. Most of them believed that he would either be a prophet or a hermit.

LUKE 1:57–80

THE BIRTH OF JESUS

The three months of Mary's absence were hard for Joseph. He wrestled with the facts in his mind. One thing was obvious, his fiancée was going to have a baby in six months' time. Everything pointed to the fact that she had been unfaithful to him. But with whom? Had she invented this story about angels?

The more Joseph thought about it the more unhappy he became. He could not marry her. But neither could he let her go through the misery of a publicly broken engagement.

Late one night, as Joseph was turning this over in his mind, he fell asleep, As he dreamed, an angel stood before him.

"Joseph, son of David," he said. "Do not be worried about marrying Mary. The baby she is to have is a gift from God. It will be a boy and you will call him Jesus, which means 'the Saviour'. He will save his people from their sins."

When Joseph woke up, he could think of nothing else. Now he knew that Mary's story was true and that he was to marry the mother of the promised Messiah. When Mary returned from visiting Elizabeth, Joseph shared his dream with her. They were married as soon as possible.

Israel was at that time an occupied country, part of the great Roman empire. Far away, in Rome, the Emperor Augustus decided to make a register of all the people in his empire. Everyone had to return to their own home town to be registered.

Joseph was a descendant of King David. This meant that he and Mary would have to travel to Bethlehem, 'City of David'. It could not be avoided, even though the baby was almost due.

After hasty preparations they set off, and a few days later they reached Bethlehem and had the chance to rest. But their problems were by no means over. The city was packed! The streets were teeming with people who, like Mary and Joseph, had come to register. But no sooner had they arrived than Mary began her labour pains. Mary knew her baby would be born very soon now. Everywhere was full. Where could they go?

Eventually, they pleaded with a local innkeeper to give them somewhere to stay. The only place he could offer was his stable. Joseph cleared a space for Mary as best he could and filled a manger (the cattle's feeding box) with clean straw.

Mary and Joseph were overjoyed when the baby boy was born. In the time-honoured custom, they washed him and rubbed his body with salt. They placed the tiny Jesus in a square of cloth, folding the corners over his sides and feet. Then they wrapped him snugly in a long bandage, and put him in the box of straw to sleep.

Meanwhile, out in the Bethlehem hills the shepherds on watch were talking quietly and keeping a sharp look out for wolves or rustlers. Suddenly, above them, the dark sky was ablaze with blinding light. Normally tough country men, they were now terrified. At the centre of this supernatural brightness an angel spoke to them. "Do not be afraid. This very night, in Bethlehem, your Saviour was born – Christ the Lord. You will find a new-born baby wrapped in cloths and lying in a manger in a stable."

The shepherds were confused as well as frightened. "The Christ? Born here? In a stable?" But before they had time to gather their wits, a mighty army of heaven's powerful angels filled the whole sky. They sang "Glory to God in the highest heaven, and peace on earth to men with whom he is pleased." The shepherds had never heard such music before.

When the angels had gone and the last echo had stopped ringing in their ears, the shepherds crowded together. "What are we waiting for?" they said to each other. "We must go into Bethlehem and find this baby." They ran down into the city and asked until they found the stable and the baby. They were even more excited when they saw the baby and realized that everything they had heard was true.

MATTHEW 1:18–25; LUKE 2:1–20

133

THE PRESENTATION AT THE TEMPLE

Strange happenings surrounded Jesus from the time he was born. Mary and Joseph had been amazed when the shepherds had come to see their baby.

Another surprise happened when Mary and Joseph took Jesus to the Temple in Jerusalem. (All Jewish parents took their first-born son to the Temple to present him to God, and to give God presents in the child's name.)

No sooner had Mary and Joseph reached the Temple steps than a strange old man walked up to them. His name was Simeon, and he lived a good, religious life. Like many other Jews, Simeon believed that God would send a Messiah – a leader to rescue the Jewish nation from its troubles. Most Jews had no idea when that leader might come; perhaps tomorrow, perhaps not for many years. But something told Simeon he would live to see the Messiah, and something led him to the Temple that day.

Mary and Joseph knew nothing of Simeon, or what went on in his mind. So Mary was astonished when the old man took her baby gently into his arms, and started praising God.

"I can die happily now, Lord," said Simeon, his voice breaking with joy. "For I have seen the saviour you have sent to the Jews – and to all the other people in the world."

Mary could hardly believe what she heard. First

It had been revealed to [Simeon] by the Holy Spirit that he would not see death until he had seen the Lord's Messiah.
Luke 2:26

the angel, then the shepherds, now this!

Simeon told her, "You will be unhappy, for many people in our country will reject Jesus."

The old man's words left Mary and Joseph rather uneasy. They knew their baby must be very special for people to say such things about him. And they were proud to think that Jesus might make people happy. But it was worrying to think that he would have enemies as well.

LUKE 2:21–38

THE WISE MEN

Even though Jesus was born in a stable, in poor and rather dirty surroundings, his birth was not unannounced. Not only did the angels appear to the shepherds when he was born, but a bright new star appeared in the sky.

Far away to the East, the star was seen by great astrologers. They were wise and knowledgeable men who made a special study of the planets and stars. When they saw this splendid new star shining in the sky, they were very excited. Their ancient scrolls told them it was a sign that a great person had been born. By the direction of the star, they judged it to be over Judea. Someone of great importance to the world must have been born in the Roman province – probably a king. As a mark of respect they decided they must see him and bring him gifts.

The wise men set off on the long journey to Jerusalem, capital city of Judea. When they arrived in Jerusalem, the city was quiet and everything appeared to be normal. There were no celebrations or dancing in the streets. In fact, no one seemed to know anything about the special birth. They made enquiries, and soon everyone in the city was talking about the astrologers and their quest. "Could it be true," they wondered, "that the real King of the Jews has been born at last?"

News of the wise men and their enquiries quickly reached the ears of Herod the Great. He had been allowed to rule Judea by the Romans and called himself King of the Jews. He was a proud, cruel man, hated by the people. When he heard the news, he was angry and worried. If the true King had been born, his own throne was in danger.

He called all his advisers together. "Where do the prophets say the Messiah is to be born?" he demanded. "The prophet Micah said that he would be born in Bethlehem," they answered.

Herod was even more worried when he heard this. Bethlehem was King David's city. A rebellion could easily be led from there. His cunning mind formed a plan. He would pretend to be as excited as the astrologers about the birth of a king. He would make

them lead him to the child. Then he would deal with him.

So Herod called the astrologers to a secret meeting at the palace. He was all smiles and welcome. "Our prophets tell us our great leader will be born in Bethlehem," he told them, in a friendly but royal way. "Go and search the city carefully. When you have found him, send me word, so that I can come and pay my respects too."

With this, the wise men set off for Bethlehem. As they began the last stage of their journey, the star that had set them on their quest reappeared in the sky. It seemed to move in front of them as they approached Bethlehem, as if leading them. They followed it. When they arrived in the city, it was not difficult to find the house where Mary and Joseph were now staying.

When the wise men saw the child, they were overjoyed. They were sure that this was the King they must greet, as the star had led them to him. They knelt down and worshipped Jesus, presenting him with the gifts they had brought – gold, frankincense and myrrh.

That night the wise men told Mary and Joseph everything that had happened to them from the time they first saw the star. They listened in wonder as Mary told them some of the amazing events surrounding the birth of the baby Jesus. The angel had said he was the Son of God.

Later, as they were preparing to return to Herod with the good news, they each had a dream in which an angel told them not to return to Herod. As they talked about their dreams the next morning, they realized how near they had come to betraying God's chosen one into the hands of a tyrant. They quickly formed their caravan again and left on the long journey home, taking a different route.

MATTHEW 2:1–12

THE FLIGHT INTO EGYPT

Soon after the wise men had hurried away, God sent an angel to Joseph in a dream. The angel's message was urgent. "Get up," he said, "take the child and his mother and go down to Egypt. Stay there until I tell you to leave. Herod will be looking for the child to kill him."

The vividness of this dream woke Joseph with a start. It was still night. Waking Mary, he told her what the angel had said. She picked up the sleeping baby. Joseph packed together their few belongings and loaded them onto their donkey. They left the house as quietly as possible and began the long journey down to Egypt. They hoped to join a caravan of travellers on the way.

It was just as well they hurried. Herod did not take long to realize that the astrologers were not returning. He was furious and flew into a terrible rage. Gone was his chance of finding out where the young child was.

But Herod was not going to give up easily. It would not be difficult for him to make sure he had no rivals. He worked out how long ago the bright, new star had appeared, so that he would know how old the baby might be. He then ordered his captains to take their troops to Bethlehem and its neighbour-hood, and to kill any boy child under the age of two. It did not matter who they were; none must be allowed to escape.

Herod's soldiers arrived in Bethlehem unannounced and unexplained. They murdered innocent, defenceless children in front of their terrified mothers. No reasons were given. Bethlehem lost all its young sons in a single day.

Meanwhile, faraway Egypt became the temporary home for the little family. Jesus' earliest years were spent in exile.

Then came news of the death of King Herod. Once more, the angel spoke to Joseph in a dream. "Take the child and his mother back to your own country," he said. "Those who tried to kill him are now dead." Joseph and Mary were glad to be able to return to their own people.

On their return, they faced the problem of where to settle. Bethlehem was too near Jerusalem, where Herod's successor, Archelaus, ruled. He was just as jealous and vicious as his father. Another dream confirmed their wish to return to Nazareth, in the north. So little Nazareth became Jesus' home as he grew up.

MATTHEW 2:13–23

An angel of the Lord appeared to Joseph in a dream, and said, "Get up, take the child and his mother and escape with them to Egypt, and stay there until I tell you; for Herod is going to search for the child to kill him."
Matthew 2:13

139

JESUS IN THE TEMPLE

The family soon settled down in Nazareth. They were happy and contented there, and Joseph worked hard at his trade as a carpenter.

Every year, the family travelled to Jerusalem for the feast of the Passover. This was the most important religious festival of the year, when Israelites looked back to the time God had freed them from captivity under the Egyptians. Jesus always went with them on this visit, but when he was twelve, the trip to Jerusalem was especially exciting for him. Twelve was the age when boys became adults and could take a full part in the religious life of the community.

Early one morning, the family set off for Jerusalem. They did not travel alone. Large groups of friends and neighbours from each town travelled together because of the dangers from robbers and wolves. Although the journey was long and tiring, it was also a great social occasion. The children especially loved it, because they could all play together on the way.

They reached Jerusalem safely, and after the Passover the caravan started on the homeward journey. It had been travelling back towards Nazareth for a whole day, when Mary and Joseph began to wonder where Jesus was. When the caravan stopped for the night, he was nowhere to be found. They thought he must be with one of his friends or another family. They went round the camp asking everyone. They searched everywhere. No one had seen him since they had set out from Jerusalem.

By this time, Mary and Joseph were frantic with worry. Could he have fallen ill and been left behind? Night had fallen and it was too late to travel back to Jerusalem. It was dangerous and they would probably miss him in the dark. They spent a sleepless night in the camp. Next morning, as dawn broke, they retraced their steps.

It was nightfall again when the weary couple arrived back in Jerusalem. Once more they had to wait until morning before continuing their desperate search. Jesus had to be somewhere. Such a special child could not disappear!

The next day they combed the bazaars and market places, asking everyone if they had seen the boy. Nobody had. They made their way towards the Temple where they had last seen him.

They could see the Temple teachers, huddled together, deep in discussion. They looked again and to their amazement there was Jesus, listening intently to every word. Now and then he would ask a question and the teachers would look at one another in astonishment. Clearly this was an unusually intelligent boy. The questions he asked were searching and he had a deep understanding for one so young.

As soon as they could attract his attention Mary and Joseph called Jesus out of the group. They hugged and kissed him because they were so delighted to find him safe. But like all mothers, Mary began to scold him. "Son, why did you do this to us?" she asked. "We have been frantic with worry trying to find you."

Jesus looked at his mother in surprise and said, "Why did you have to look for me? Didn't you know that I would be in my father's house?"

Mary was taken aback at this. She could see he was perfectly serious, and she struggled to understand what he meant. The next day, the family joined another caravan, heading north, and no more was said about the event. But Mary and Joseph thought about Jesus' words. They realized that their son had greater work to do than be a carpenter all his life.

LUKE 2:41–51

"Why did you search for me?" he said. "Did you not know that I was bound to be in my Father's house?"
Luke 2:49

JESUS AS A BOY

After the trip to Jerusalem, the family settled down once more to life in Nazareth. Joseph picked up his tools again and continued his work as a carpenter and builder. He worked hard and his business prospered, and he began to teach Jesus the skills he had learnt over the years.

Jesus grew up, a normal, healthy boy, and he enjoyed helping Joseph in his workshop. Joseph

taught him how to choose the best wood for each job, how to cut and plane it, how to make solid joints and work the wood to a good finish. Jesus, 'the carpenter's son' as he became known in the district, was good at the trade Joseph taught him. He was pleasant, honest, hard-working and modest. He had a strong personality, but with a wise head on his young shoulders. Everyone he mixed with liked him and was impressed by the kind of life he lived. And Jesus' heavenly father, God, knew his every thought and action. He, too, was pleased with what he saw.

As Jesus grew older he grew even more in wisdom and in strength. He stayed with his family and worked hard for them until he was thirty years old, by which time he was ready to go out into the world on his great mission.

LUKE 2:40, 52

As Jesus grew he advanced in wisdom and in favour with God and men.
Luke 2:52

JOHN BAPTIZES JESUS

While Jesus was still working with Joseph in the carpenter's shop, God's call came to John, the son of Zechariah. He left his home and went out into the desert. There he lived alone, spending time praying and preparing himself for his great mission.

It was a hard living under the baking sun, in a place where little water or food was to be found. John ate what he could find in the desert, living off grasshopper-like locusts and the occasional honeycomb from the nests of wild bees.

Before long John felt that God wanted him to move on. God had given him strength and powerful words to say. Immediately, he went on to the region around the river Jordan where he began to preach.

His message was simple and direct. The people must repent, turn from their evil ways and ask God to forgive them. His preaching was so powerful, that crowds came to hear him. Many of the people realized that God was not happy with the way they were living and they were deeply sorry. John baptized these people. He took them into the river Jordan and plunged them under the water. It was a public sign that they were washing away the wrong they had done and that they were now going to live new lives.

John baptized people wherever he went, and so he became known as John the Baptist. People from all the nearby towns and villages flocked to hear him preach. Some of the religious leaders came out to hear him, too. John turned on them: they were so religious yet they were so proud. He called them a 'family of snakes'. This made enemies for John.

John's teaching was practical and down-to-earth. He taught people to care for one another and to share their goods. "If anyone has two coats," he said, looking round at his audience, "give one of them to someone who has none." He told the hated tax-collectors to stop swindling people. He even spoke to the occupation troops of the Roman army: "No bullying – and be content with your pay!"

Soon, rumours began to spread. "John is the Messiah! He is the man to lead us against our rulers." But John put a stop to such talk. "I baptize you with water," he said, "but someone who is far greater than I am is coming. He is so great that I am not worthy enough to undo the straps on his sandals. He will baptize you with the Holy Spirit and with fire." By this, he meant that the Messiah would have God's power to clean people's minds and hearts.

By this time, Jesus also knew that he must begin God's work. He travelled down from his home town to see John by the river Jordan. When John saw Jesus, he knew immediately who he was. All his life had been leading up to this moment. Quietly, Jesus stepped forward and asked to be baptized. John was shocked. Jesus had done nothing wrong. He did not need a ritual washing.

"But I need to be baptized by you," John said, "not the other way round." Jesus replied, "Let it be like this for now. By doing this, we shall be doing what God wants." Jesus wanted to go through the ceremony as a way of showing that he had accepted God's plan for his life. He was ready to begin the work he had been sent to do. So John agreed and they both stepped down into the river Jordan.

John lowered Jesus into the water and then raised him up again. Suddenly, as Jesus stood up, the sky seemed to open above them, and the Spirit of God descended on him. He heard a voice from heaven saying, "This is my own dear son, with whom I am well pleased."

MATTHEW 3; MARK 1:1–11; LUKE 3:1–22; JOHN 1:19–34

And a voice came from heaven: "You are my beloved Son; in you I take delight."
Mark 1:11

JESUS IN THE DESERT

When Jesus left John the Baptist, he was ready for the great mission ahead of him. He was going to need the spiritual strength that God's Spirit had given him, because he was about to undergo one of the toughest tests of his life. He left the river and went into the bleak desert country west of the Jordan valley. It was an unfriendly place, sweltering hot in the day and freezing cold at night. It could be dangerous too. Wolves and lions hunted there and scorpions and snakes hid in the rocks.

Jesus was out in the desert for forty days and forty nights. He ate no food at all. He spent his time praying to God, his father, and thinking about how he was to begin his work. By the fortieth day, Jesus was exhausted and very hungry.

It was not only lack of food and comfort that Jesus faced. God's spirit had led him there for the first encounter with his deadly enemy, the Devil. This is the spiritual battle that always rages between good and evil. The Prince of Evil, as the Devil is sometimes called, knew that Jesus had come to destroy his power. Yet there was a chance that Jesus could be tempted away from God's will and persuaded not to trust him.

"Jesus," the tempter whispered into his mind, "if you are the Son of God, you could turn these stones into bread."

"No," said Jesus, "God has said, 'Man needs more than bread to live on, he needs to trust every word God says.'"

The Devil tried again. Perhaps he could make Jesus misuse his power to impress the people. "If you really are the Son of God," he whispered again, "you could throw yourself off the highest part of the Temple and not be hurt. The scriptures say 'God will send his angels to keep you from harm. They will not let you so much as stub your foot on the rocks.'"

Jesus imagined what would happen. God's son could not be killed and the people would all follow him. But for the wrong reasons. "God also says 'You shall not put the Lord God to the test.'" he replied, firmly.

Finally, the Devil decided to show Jesus what real power was like. This time he made Jesus think of all the kingdoms in the world, their riches and glory. It was as if he could see them all from the peak of a very high mountain. Now it was no longer subtle temptation. "There," he said, "all that is yours to do with what you will. All you have to do is kneel down and worship me." Jesus summoned all his energy. In a powerful voice, full of command, he said "Satan, get out of here. The scriptures say: 'You shall worship the Lord your God, and serve only him.'"

Defeated and bitter, the Devil left Jesus. When he had gone, angels came from God to support the frail but victorious Jesus. He had passed the first, great test of his career.

MATTHEW 4:1–11; MARK 1:12–13; LUKE 4:1–13

Jesus was then led by the Spirit into the wilderness, to be tempted by the devil.

For forty days and nights he fasted, and at the end of them he was famished. The tempter approached him and said, "If you are the Son of God, tell these stones to become bread." Jesus answered, "Scripture says, 'Man is not to live on bread alone, but on every word that comes from the mouth of God.'"
Matthew 4:1–4

JESUS CALLS
SIMON AND ANDREW

Simon and Andrew had rowed out onto the great lake called the Sea of Galilee. They had cast their fishing net, and now they were wading ashore to haul it in.

It was hard to walk thigh-deep through water over a stony lake bed, as they dragged their heavy load up to the beach. Yet they knew they must do this again and again before they caught enough fish.

It was difficult, badly paid work and they worked long hours, but at least it gave them a living.

The brothers were nearing the shore when they glanced up and saw a man approaching. His calm, smiling face made them feel oddly at peace. The stranger was Jesus.

His first words took them both by surprise. "Come with me," he invited. "I'll teach you how to fish for the souls of men."

If anyone else had said that, the brothers might have laughed and thought him mad. But Jesus had a way of making people listen to him. The brothers felt they must obey him. They dropped their net, and strode after Jesus without so much as a backward glance at their boat.

It was the same with James and John, a bit further up the beach. They were sitting mending their nets when Jesus called them to follow him too. These brothers also dropped what they were doing.

All four men – and later others as well – set out on a brand new life as Jesus' chosen disciples.

These followers no longer earned their living by fishing or other everyday work. From now on they helped Jesus as he travelled from town to town, healing and blessing the sick and preaching a powerful message to great crowds.

Jesus announced a new Kingdom – but not the independent Jewish kingdom that most Jews had been hoping for. What Jesus meant was a new 'Kingdom' in people's minds; a new way of thinking and feeling about people and God.

MATTHEW 4:18–25; MARK 1:16–20; LUKE 5:1–11

A WEDDING AT CANA

A wedding was being held in Cana, a town in Galilee. It was a splendid affair. Jesus, his mother and his disciples had been invited. Everyone was enjoying themselves. The bridegroom's house was packed with friends and relatives of the bride and groom. There was a great feast with music, dancing and singing. People made speeches and told each other jokes and the feast continued well into the night.

Everything seemed to be going well, when Jesus' mother, Mary, came over to her son, looking worried. "The wine has run out," she whispered.

"Why turn to me," he said, gently. "My time has not yet come for miracles." Jesus knew his mother wanted him to work a miracle. She was always sure he could do anything he pleased. But he knew he must not misuse his powers. However, Mary thought he would do something for his friend. She went out to where the servants were standing. They were wondering whether to tell the steward about the wine. He was a friend of the bridegroom and was in charge of the feast. "Here comes my son," Mary said to the servants. "Follow his instructions carefully."

Six large stone jars were standing in the corner. They were used to hold water for the ceremonial washing of the guests' hands and feet. They were enormous, each one could hold between eighty and one hundred and twenty litres. Jesus gathered the servants together and said: "Fill these jars with water." They did exactly as he said, filling them to the brim. In the meantime, the guests were getting restless. A rumour was spreading that the wine had run out.

Jesus said to the servants, "Now pour some of the water into a serving jug and take it to the steward." The servant handed it to the steward who looked at it and took a sip. The servant waited, not knowing what to expect.

The steward's face beamed with pleasure. He called the bridegroom over. "Everyone serves the best wine first and then they bring out the ordinary wine," he said, "but I see you've saved the best wine till last!"

The new wine was quickly served to the guests and the feast continued as if nothing had happened. Only Mary, the servants and the disciples knew that Jesus had performed this miracle.

JOHN 2:1–11

Jesus said to the servants, "Fill the jars with water," and they filled them to the brim. "Now draw some off," he ordered, "and take it to the master of the feast"; and they did so. The master tasted the water now turned into wine, not knowing its source, though the servants who had drawn the water knew.
John 2:7–9

THE SOWER

As Jesus walked down to the lake of Galilee one bright sunny morning the word spread about – Jesus is here! Soon a large crowd had gathered, waiting to hear what he had to say. The crowd grew so big that Jesus borrowed one of the fishermen's boats moored in the lake's shallows. Jesus stood in the prow of the boat and talked about what he had come to earth to do.

He began, as usual, by telling them a story. "There was once a farmer who decided to sow corn in one of his fields. As he scattered the seed, some of it fell on the stony path and the birds swooped down to pick it up. Other seed fell on the rocky ground where there was little soil. The seed sprouted but it only managed to make shallow roots because the soil was not deep. As soon as the sun came up the tender shoots withered because the plants were not strong. Some of the seed fell among thorn bushes which grew up quicker than the corn and choked it before it had a chance to flourish. But some of the seed fell on good, rich soil and the plants grew into healthy corn, producing thirty, sixty or even a hundred grains."

The crowd listened enthralled to all Jesus had to teach them. They would never forget the stories, but what did they mean? Little groups in the crowd were discussing them long after Jesus had left.

Later the close circle of friends of Jesus gathered round him and asked him to explain what he meant by the story of the sower.

Jesus told them that the seed was like the message he had come to give. "The seeds are my words. Those people who hear what I have to say but fail to understand it are like the stony path. The evil one takes the message away before it can bear fruit.

"The rocky ground stands for those who accept

the truth of my message as soon as they hear it, but are not prepared to be my followers. As soon as things become difficult for them, they give up.

"The thorn bushes are like the people who believe me but their busy lives and their love of money and possessions choke the message so that it does not make a real difference to the way they live.

"The good fertile soil stands for those who understand and accept my teaching and live it out in their lives. Some will do great things for me, others can do less, but they will all be fruitful like the ears of corn."

To show that some people would respond to him and some would not, Jesus told another story.

"A farmer sowed his field with good seeds of wheat. Then one night, when everyone was asleep, his great rival sneaked into the field and sowed weeds among the wheat. As you would imagine, the wheat and the weeds grew up together. The farm workers were puzzled. 'Where have all these weeds come from?' they asked the farmer. 'You only sowed good seed.'

"'My enemy did it,' answered the farmer angrily.

'Do you want us to pull up the weeds?' the farm workers asked. 'No, you might pull up the wheat with them. Wait till harvest time. Then, when they are fully grown, the harvesters will have no trouble in separating them. Then they can pull up the weeds and burn them and only the wheat will be left.'"

Jesus explained that this is what will happen to people at the end of the world. They will be judged as to whether they truly belong to God, or to the evil one.

Jesus told a different story to explain the same point.

"Fishermen throw their nets out into the lake and pull in all kinds of fish – some good to eat and others that are never eaten. It is not until the net is full and they pull it into shore that they can divide the good fish from the bad. The good fish go into buckets, but the others are thrown away. It will be the same at the end of the age," Jesus said. "God's angels will sort out God's followers from the others."

MATTHEW 13:1–50; MARK 4:1–20; LUKE 8:4–15

"A sower went out to sow. And as he sowed, some of the seed fell along the footpath; and the birds came and ate it up. Some fell on rocky ground, where it had little soil, and it sprouted quickly because it had no depth of earth; but when the sun rose it was scorched, and as it had no root it withered away."
Matthew 13:3–6

153

JOHN IS BEHEADED

John the Baptist lay in chains in the dungeons of the fortress-like palace of King Herod Antipas at Machaerus in the south of Perea. He had been put there by King Herod at the insistence of his wife Herodias. John had told Herod many times that he should not have married her, because she was his half-brother's wife and it was against Jewish law. So Herodias hated John. She wanted him killed, but Herod could not bring himself to do it. He knew that John was a holy man and he did fear God. John was also very popular. To kill him would ruin Herod's delicate relationship with the people. So John was locked up safely out of Herod's way and no decision had yet been made about his future.

Meanwhile, upstairs in the magnificent palace banqueting hall, Herod was holding a great party. It was his birthday. Many important people were there – top government officials, the military chiefs of staff and the leading citizens of the province of Perea. The hall was filled with laughter, music and dancing. Herod was enjoying his birthday party immensely.

Late in the evening, Salome, Herodias' daughter by her first marriage, offered to dance. This was a special treat for Herod and his guests, for Salome could dance beautifully. Everyone cheered and clapped as she glided onto the floor of the banqueting hall. How well she danced! No one had seen such dancing for years. Herod could be tough and heartless, but he could also be sentimental at times. He was delighted that Salome had danced for him and his guests. When she had finished, and the applause had died down, he called her to him.

In front of everyone he declared, "Tell me what you want and you will have it. Anything you ask is yours, even up to half my kingdom," he said. All the guests roared their approval.

Salome did not know what to do or what to ask for. Excitedly, she rushed up to her mother, Herodias. "Mother," she said, "what shall I say?"

Herodias saw her chance. She hated John the Baptist for the things he said, but without Herod's approval there was nothing she could do. Here, at last, was a way for her to be rid of him. "Herod says you can have anything you want," she told her daughter. "Tell him you want John the Baptist's head," she hissed, "on a plate." Salome looked hard at her mother. Then she ran back to King Herod.

The hall was quiet as she approached her step-father. What was she going to ask for? A horse? Expensive jewels? Money? Perhaps she would take up his offer of a part of the kingdom?

Looking straight at King Herod, she demanded: "I want the head of John the Baptist on a plate." There were horrified gasps. Could this be true? Salome, the beautiful dancer, wanted the holy man John executed? Herod was desolate. He knew immediately who was responsible for tricking him.

Herod had no wish to kill John; he quite liked him, although he was rather uncomfortable to be with. John never feared to tell Herod things about himself that he did not want to hear. He seemed to be an honest man, and what if God really was with him?

But Herod was trapped. He had made a solemn promise to Salome in front of all the guests. He could not break his word. Finally, it was pride, not conscience, that won. And, like his father, who had killed all the small boys in Bethlehem years before, he was concerned for himself and his survival.

With a heavy heart, he called one of the palace guards and ordered him to go down to the dungeons to carry out the execution. The guard unlocked John the Baptist's cell and then, with his sword, he cut off the prisoner's head.

The birthday guests were silent as Herod's guard strode back into the hall, holding John's head, still dripping blood. He put it onto a silver tray and presented it to Salome. The girl silently handed the gift to her mother.

The next day, news of John's murder was brought to his followers. They were sad and angry. As quickly as they could, they came to Machaerus and took John's body away to give it a proper burial. Then they hurried off to tell Jesus what had happened. Jesus was full of sorrow at his friend's death.

John's death marked a turning point for Jesus. John had been called to prepare for God's Son. Now John's followers joined Jesus, whose work had just begun.

The shame of John's murder never left Herod. He was haunted by thoughts of the innocent, holy man.

Later, when he heard of all the miraculous and wonderful things Jesus was doing, he was frightened. He had been told that it was John the Baptist returned from the dead. "I had his head cut off, but he has come back to life!"

Three years later, Herod was to meet Jesus face to face, just before Jesus was put to death. Those three years were to be the most eventful and significant the world has ever seen.

MATTHEW 14:1–12; MARK 6:14–29

THE SERMON ON THE MOUNT

One day Jesus took his followers up the slopes of a large hill. There, he outlined the main points of his teaching – the things he wanted them to remember and put into practice in their daily lives.

"Happy are the poor, the humble, the kind, the peacemakers, and those who try to be good and just, those who are sad and those who are persecuted. For people like these will find their reward in the Kingdom of Heaven.

"So do not worry if people insult you or make up lies about you because you have followed me. You can still be happy. A great reward is waiting for you in heaven. And remember, God's greatest prophets were treated in the same way.

"Your goodness should be as obvious as a city on a hill. After all, no one lights a lamp and puts it under a bowl, do they? They put it on a lampstand, so that it will provide light for everyone in the house.

"Do not think that I have come to abolish the Law and teachings of the prophets," he said. "No, I am making it clearer for you. But you must follow the spirit rather than the letter of the Law."

Jesus went on: "The Law says that anyone who commits murder will face trial. I am telling you, even if you are angry with someone else you will have to answer for it to God himself. So if you are about to worship the Lord and remember that you have wronged someone – stop! Put the matter right immediately. Then you can worship God.

"You know that in the old days people used to say, 'Take an eye for an eye and a tooth for a tooth.' I say do not try to get your own back on anyone who has wronged you. If someone asks you for something, do not hesitate, give it to him. If a person wants to borrow something, lend it to him. If a Roman soldier makes you carry his heavy pack for a mile, offer to carry it for another mile as well."

MATTHEW 5:1–26; LUKE 6:20–38

"Blessed are the poor in spirit;
the kingdom of Heaven is theirs.
Blessed are the sorrowful;
they shall find consolation.
Blessed are the gentle;
they shall have the earth for their
    possession.
Blessed are those who hunger and
    thirst to see right prevail;
they shall be satisfied.
Blessed are those who show mercy;
mercy shall be shown to them.
Blessed are those whose hearts are
    pure;
they shall see God.
Blessed are the peacemakers;
they shall be called God's children.
Blessed are those who are persecuted
    in the cause of right;
the kingdom of Heaven is theirs.
Matthew 5:3–10

The House Built on a Rock

As the Sermon on the Mount drew to a close, Jesus told a story to everyone gathered round. "So," he concluded, "those of you who have listened carefully and will start putting my teaching into practice, are like the man who built his house on good foundations. The man decided to do it properly. He wanted the house to last for a long time. He drew up detailed plans so that the construction would be strong. But knowing that the most secure structure in the world is no use if the foundations are not solid, he searched around until he found a plot with a good firm bedrock.

"'This is the place to build,' the man said to himself. And then he began the long slow business of digging foundations for his house. Once this was done, the building went up in no time. Eventually, having secured the roof and made sure that everything was safe, he moved in.

"A little while later another man arrived. He too wanted to build his own house. He wandered about until he found a nice plot of land with a good view. He did not bother to test the ground. He was keen to get on with the building. He could see his neighbour, labouring away at the rock, and he congratulated himself on finding a plot that was so much softer and easier to work. As you can imagine, the second man's house was finished first. With a superior smile and a wave at his neighbour, the man moved his family and possessions in.

"Not long after both houses had been completed there was a terrible rain storm. It poured down day after day until the rivers became swollen and broke their banks. Fierce gales blew and battered against the houses.

"The first man was not worried. He knew he had built the house as well as he could. Sure enough it stood firm throughout the storm because he had built secure foundations on rock. The second man began to worry as soon as the floods began to rise. The water spread quickly in the sandy soil and the ground soon became unstable. The house began to shake. Then, with a rending crash, the house caved in. In a matter of seconds, all his work was destroyed."

Jesus looked steadily at his disciples and the surrounding crowd. But he said no more. The meaning was plain. They, in turn, looked at Jesus. This man spoke as if he really knew what he was talking about.

MATTHEW 7:24–29; LUKE 6:46–49

"So whoever hears these words of mine and acts on them is like a man who had the sense to build his house on rock."
Matthew 7:24

THE WEDDING FEAST

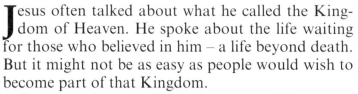

Jesus often talked about what he called the Kingdom of Heaven. He spoke about the life waiting for those who believed in him – a life beyond death. But it might not be as easy as people would wish to become part of that Kingdom.

One story Jesus told was about a wedding reception.

"Once there was a king who prepared a wonderful wedding feast for his son. He sent out servants to tell all those who had been invited to come to the feast, but none of them seemed interested. So the king sent

more servants to remind the guests about the feast. But the guests ignored the king's invitation and carried on working on their farms. Some became angry with the king's servants and attacked and killed them.

"In the end the king became extremely angry. 'That's it. They've lost their opportunity! I won't ask them again,' he said. He then sent his servants out into the city streets and country lanes and told them to invite anyone, whoever they were, to come to the feast. Soon the great hall of the palace was filled with people.

"All except one man came dressed as they had been asked. This man had not bothered to get ready. He had wandered in as if he could not care less about the king and his invitation. The king noticed the man and asked him how he had got in without being properly dressed. The man refused to answer. Without more ado, the king had the man thrown out of the palace because he had taken no notice of the king's wishes."

To show how the Kingdom on earth would grow and grow, Jesus used two different pictures.

Teaching about the Kingdom was like a man sowing mustard seed in a field. In Palestine these tiny seeds grew into trees sometimes as much as five metres tall. Jesus said that, as a result of the seeds he had sown, the Kingdom of God would grow like a great plant – so tall that birds could nest in it.

Jesus also talked about the influence God's people would have on the world. He said they would act like a small amount of yeast mixed in with as much as forty litres of flour. Before long the live yeast would make the dough rise. In the same way God's Kingdom in people's hearts and minds would spread all over the world.

MATTHEW 13:31–33; 22:1–14; MARK 4:30–32; LUKE 13:18–21

You Cannot Serve Two Masters

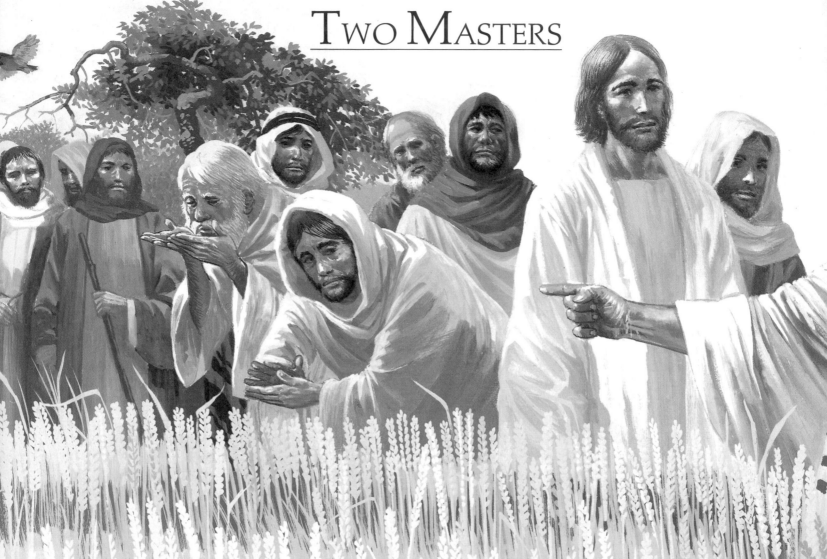

Exactly as they do today, the people in the days of Jesus spent a lot of their time and energy worrying. The farmers worried about the harvest, and the fishermen worried about the size of their catch.

"Do not be so concerned about getting rich on earth," Jesus told them. "Down here moths could ruin your rich clothes, your beautiful metalware could rust and burglars steal your money and jewels. It would be much better if you thought about gaining wealth in heaven. The rewards you will be given in heaven cannot be damaged or stolen."

"You have to decide. Either you serve God or you become a slave to money and the good life. Remember this: you cannot serve two masters.

"This is why I am telling you not to worry about food or drink or what you wear. If you serve God you need have nothing to fear."

Then pointing to the birds that fluttered and chirped happily nearby, Jesus said with a smile, "Just look at these little creatures. They do not sow seeds or harvest crops. They do not have storerooms and barns. Yet God, your Father in heaven, looks after them. In the market place you can buy five sparrows for two pennies. But God does not forget a single one of them. Are you not worth more than them? Why, even the hairs on your head have all been counted.

"What good does worrying do anyway? Can any of you live even a day longer by getting yourself into a state about it? And then there are the clothes you

wear. Look at these beautiful wild flowers. They do not work or make clothes for themselves, but even great King Solomon himself, with all his fabulous wealth, never had clothes so fine as these! Just think if God is in control of such things as wild grass – plants that are here today and gone tomorrow – is he not able to make sure that you have clothes to wear? You have not got much faith in him have you?

"So do not worry so much. Remember, your Father in heaven knows what you need. Instead, concern yourself about important things – about how God wants you to live."

Another day, Jesus was walking through the cornfields. It was a Saturday, the Sabbath or Holy Day of the Jews. His friends, who were hungry, began picking corn, rubbing it in their hands and eating it.

"Look," said the Pharisees, "why are your followers doing what is not allowed on the Sabbath?" According to the strict letter of the Law plucking was regarded as reaping and rubbing the corn was threshing. So, to the Pharisees, Jesus' disciples were guilty of working on the Sabbath.

Jesus replied: "Have you not read in the scriptures what King David did when he and his men were hungry? He went into the House of God and he and his men ate the special bread that only the priests were allowed to eat. The Sabbath," Jesus went on, "was made for man, not man for the Sabbath." By this he meant that the Sabbath was made to help men and women.

MATTHEW 6:19–34; 12:1–8; LUKE 12:32–34

THE FRIEND AT MIDNIGHT

In Jesus' time most people were in great awe of God. They thought of him as the mighty creator who sat in judgement over his people. True, he had helped the Jewish nation many times in the past. But they thought of him as so powerful and far above the concerns of ordinary people, that he seemed unapproachable. They would never use his name; it was so holy.

Jesus knew that God the creator was all of these things, but that this was only half of the picture. By his life and teaching Jesus showed that God was approachable. He taught that God could be thought of as a father. More than that, he could be a friend. Praying to God need not be like addressing a king or prime minister. It was more like talking to someone you know. If you needed something, you could ask for it and keep on asking, sure of being heard.

Jesus told the story. "Suppose one of your friends turned up and asked to stay with you for the night, and suppose you did not have any food in the house. Even if it was midnight, you would go to a friend's house and say, 'I've got an unexpected guest. Could you lend me some bread? We are completely out.' Then just suppose your friend said, 'Don't bother me now! The door is locked and we are all in bed. You will have to wait until tomorrow!' Well, you know perfectly well that, if you kept on asking, your friend would get out of bed and find some bread for you.

"It is the same when you pray to God. If you ask, you will receive. If you are searching, you will find the answer in the end. Knock on a door and it will be opened. That is what your heavenly Father is like.

"Some of you are fathers yourselves. If your son asked you for bread, you would not give him a hard stone, would you? If he asked you for a fish, would you give him a snake? Of course, you would not. As selfish as you often are, you still love your children enough to give them only the best. How much more then will the Father in heaven give good things to those who ask him?"

Some time later, Jesus told a story to show how important it is to keep on praying and not to get discouraged if nothing seems to happen straight away.

"There was once a small town judge. He had no reverence for God and absolutely no respect for his fellow townspeople. But he had a lot of power and influence in the local community. One day a widow came to see him. She had a grievance against someone who had cheated her. She knew her rights, and wanted the judge to help her win her case. The judge was not interested. But the widow kept coming back, pleading for her rights. Each time the judge would do nothing. This went on for a long time until finally, fed up with the widow, the judge said to himself, 'I pride myself in caring for neither God nor man, but I am going to have to do something about this case. Unless I make a judgement against the man who cheated the widow, I will get no peace at all!'

"So, worn down by the widow's persistence, the judge acted. The woman went away satisfied and justice had been done.

"Now," Jesus told his disciples, "think about my story. If the judge, who was corrupt and inhumane, did the right thing in the end, what do you think God will do when his people cry out to him for help day and night? He will not be slow to answer them."

Prayer was very important to Jesus. He prayed often, talking to his Father as any son would, bringing to him the difficulties and joys of the life he had come to live. Many of his prayers are recorded in the Gospels.

Just before one of Jesus' most astounding miracles – when he brought his friend Lazarus back to life – Jesus looked up to the skies and said very simply, "I thank you, Father, that you hear my prayer. I know that you always listen to me, but I want other people to be quite certain that you have sent me."

Shortly before Jesus himself was put to death, he asked God, his Father, to look after his friends. He prayed, "Holy Father! Keep them safe by the power of your name, the name you gave me. May they be one, just as you and I are one."

Earlier, when Jesus knew for sure that his death was coming, he breathed a prayer to God, preparing himself for what he knew he must go through. He said, "Now my heart is heavy. What shall I pray? Shall I pray 'Father, do not let this happen to me?' But that is why I came – so that I could go through this time of suffering. No, I will pray, 'Father, bring glory to your name'."

Even when he was moments away from death, nailed by his hands and feet to a cross, Jesus was able to ask God's pardon for those who had put him there. "Forgive them, Father," he whispered, "they do not know what they are doing."

To Jesus, prayer was as natural as life itself. It was not a religious ritual, nor was it something to use to impress people, as the Pharisees did. He told people, "When you pray, do not be like the religious hypocrites who love to stand up in places of worship, or even on street corners and pray where everyone can see them. Instead, go to your room and close the door. Then pray to God your Father in secret and he will reward you. Do not use lots of meaningless, religious-sounding words. Some people think that God will hear them because their prayers are long and impressive. God already knows what you need, even before you ask."

Jesus gave his disciples an example of the kind of prayer he meant. "It is best to pray for something simple like this," he said. "Father, may your name be kept holy, may your Kingdom come. Give us day by day, the food we need. Forgive us our sins as we forgive everyone who has done us wrong and do not bring us to hard testing."

MATTHEW *6*:9–13; *7*:7–11; *11*:25–27; LUKE *10*:21–22; *11*:1–13; *18*:1–8; JOHN *11*:41–42

At one place after Jesus had been praying, one of his disciples said, "Lord, teach us to pray, as John taught his disciples." He answered. "When you pray, say,
"Father, may your name be hallowed;
*   your kingdom come.*
Give us each day our daily bread.
And forgive us our sins,
*   for we too forgive all who have done*
*   us wrong.*
And do not put us to the test."
Luke 11:1–4

Jesus and Children

Jesus loved children. More than once he used them to illustrate the kind of trust that adults should have in God. But the followers of Jesus and the people who came to listen to him felt that children got in the way.

On one occasion when Jesus was teaching a gathering of people, some parents brought their children to him, asking Jesus to place his hands on them and bless them. But the disciples tried to protect Jesus. "Clear off!" they said. "The master has got better things to do than spend time with children."

But Jesus was angry. "Stop!" he said. "Let the children come to me. The Kingdom of God belongs to children like these." Looking at the eager, trusting faces of the children he said, "Let me assure you, anyone who does not receive God's teaching in the trusting way these children do, will not enter his Kingdom." Then gathering the children into his arms he blessed each one of them.

One Sabbath Jesus went to a dinner party at the home of a leading Pharisee. As people arrived, he observed them carefully. Some of the guests automatically went to the best places and sat down, sure that they were the most important people in the room. When everyone was seated, Jesus started talking to them all. He said: "When someone invites you to a wedding or to a dinner, do not sit down in the best place. You never know, someone more important then you might arrive. Your host may have to ask you to move down. Just think how embarrassing that would be.

"Instead, take the lowest place first of all. Then the chances are, your host will say, 'Don't sit there! Come up here my friend and take this seat.' Then you will be honoured in the sight of all the guests. In the end humble, modest people will be given positions of greatness and the people who think themselves great will be nowhere."

Jesus then turned to his host and said: "When you give a dinner, do not invite your close friends, your relatives or your rich neighbours. They are able to invite you back and you will be repaid for giving them dinner. When you give a party, invite people with no money, the disabled or those who do not normally get out. They will not be able to repay you for what you have done and your reward will come later, in heaven."

Jesus was well aware that one day he would have to leave his disciples and he tried to prepare them for the time when they would have to stand alone. He told them that they were to act as God's servants. "A faithful and wise servant is the one that his master can trust with the whole household while he is away. He will be expected to run the house and take charge of the other servants. Everything will be fine for that servant if he is doing his job well when his master returns. But woe betide him if the master finds that he has abused the privileges he was given. Suppose he thinks, 'The master is going to be away a long time. I'll take advantage of his absence.' He beats the other servants and eats all the master's best food. Imagine what would happen if the master suddenly returned. The servant would be punished and given the sack.

"To be God's servant is an honour. Much will be expected of those who are given such a task."

Servants in Jesus' time did not have an easy life. Jesus used them as an example of the kind of hard-working service that God demands. "Suppose one of your servants has been out all day ploughing the fields and looking after the sheep. When he comes in you do not say, 'You can have a rest now.' You say, 'I would like my supper now. Please get it ready for me, and then serve at table. After that you can go and have your own meal.' That is what a servant expects. It is the same with you. When you have done all God has told you to do, think to yourself, 'I am one of God's servants.'"

On the same subject of doing God's will, Jesus put a question to the Temple teachers: "What do you

They brought children for him to touch. The disciples rebuked them, but when Jesus saw it he was indignant, and said to them, "Let the children come to me; do not try to stop them; for the kingdom of God belongs to such as these. Truly I tell you: whoever does not accept the kingdom of God like a child will never enter it." And he put his arms round them, laid his hands on them, and blessed them. Mark 10:13–16

think about this?" he said. "There was once a man who had two sons. To the elder boy he said, 'Son, I want you to work in the vineyard today.'

"'Oh, Father, I don't want to,' the son replied. But then, when he had had time to think about it, he knew that he really ought to help his father. So, without saying anything, he made his way to the vineyard and started work.

"Meanwhile the father went to the younger son and told him the same thing. 'Certainly, father,' said his son, 'I'll do that.' But as soon as his father left, the boy did something else.

"Which one of the two sons did what his father wanted?" Jesus asked. "The older one," came the reply. "Good intentions are absolutely no use," Jesus told his audience. "It is what you actually do that is important."

MATTHEW *19*:13–15; *21*:28–32; *24*:45–51; MARK *10*:13–16; LUKE *12*:41–48; *14*:7–14; *17*:7–10

PETER THE ROCK

Jesus loved all his disciples. Where he went they followed, helping to cure the sick and to control the crowds that came to see Jesus.

But Jesus wanted to know what the disciples thought of him.

One day he asked his disciples, "Who do men say I am?" They replied, "Some say you are John the Baptist; others say Elijah; others, Jeremiah or one of the prophets."

So people thought he might be one of God's dead but famous messengers come alive again.

Then Jesus asked them outright, "But who do *you* think I am?"

There was a short pause. Most of the disciples were not sure what to say. But Simon, who was also called Peter, had no doubts. "You are the Christ, the chosen one, the Son of God," he declared.

Jesus smiled. "Bless you Simon," he said. "Only my Father in heaven can have told you that. Your other name, Peter, means 'rock' and I shall make you the rock on which I shall build my church. I shall give you the keys of the Kingdom of Heaven, with the power to lock or to open its doors."

Jesus then went on to explain to his disciples that he had to go to Jerusalem and undergo terrible suffering at the hands of the elders, chief priests and scribes. He said that he would be put to death, but that he would rise from the dead on the third day.

Peter was deeply upset and took hold of Jesus and cried, "This must not happen!" But Jesus was angry with him. "Get behind me Satan! You are seeing things through man's eyes rather then through God's!" Jesus was concerned as he saw that Peter still did not fully understand his mission.

About a week later, Jesus took Peter, James and John up a high mountain to pray.

As Jesus prayed, the disciples fell asleep. Then Jesus became transfigured – his face shone like the sun and his clothes became a brilliant, dazzling white. The disciples woke up to see this, and then to their further astonishment Moses and Elijah appeared and talked to Jesus.

Peter did not know what to think or do, then he said to Jesus, "It is so good that we are all here together, shall I make three tents – one for you, one for Moses and one for Elijah?" But he had hardly finished speaking, when a bright cloud suddenly overshadowed them and a voice called from the cloud: "This is my beloved Son, of whom I am well pleased, listen to him."

The disciples sank down to the ground in fear at hearing this voice. But Jesus said kindly: "Do not be afraid." And when the disciples raised their eyes, no one was there, but Jesus.

MATTHEW *16*:13–28 TO *17*:1–8; MARK *8*:27–38 TO *9*:1–8; LUKE *9*:18–36

"And I say to you: you are Peter, the Rock; and on this rock I will build my church, and the powers of death shall never conquer it."
Matthew 16:18

THE GOOD SAMARITAN

One day an expert in the laws of the Bible stood up at a meeting and asked Jesus this question:

"Teacher, what must I do to win a place in heaven forever?"

Jesus knew the man was testing him, to see if what he taught fitted in with the laws laid down long ago in the Bible.

Jesus was not to be caught out. He asked another question in return: "What does the law of Moses say you should do?"

The man replied, "It says you must love God with all your heart, soul, strength and mind. And you must love your neighbour as much as you love yourself."

"That's right," said Jesus.

But the expert pretended not to know quite what this meant. "Who exactly *is* my neighbour?" was his next question.

Jesus felt he could best explain by telling the following story:

"A Jew was making a trip from Jerusalem to Jericho. Part of the road was rough, steep and dangerous. Robbers were likely to lay in wait for lonely travellers here.

"And that is exactly what happened. One moment the Jew was quietly plodding along in the hot sun. The next instant bandits leapt out from behind a rock and attacked him. They stole his money, ripped the clothes off his back and beat him up. Then they ran off, leaving him lying half dead by the road.

"The wretched man was bleeding and bruised from head to toe, and a blow on the head had left him almost knocked out. For a time all he heard was a ringing noise in his head and the buzzing of flies.

"Then came the sound of footsteps approaching. His eyes opened wide with fear – maybe it was the robbers returning to finish him off.

"He sighed with relief to see a Jewish priest coming – help at last.

"Or was it? The priest took one look at the wretch

sprawled by the road and covered in blood and dust. Then he crossed over to avoid him, and walked on quickly. Moses' law said priests must not touch blood.

"Soon after, along came one of the priests' helpers. He, at least, paused and looked down at the injured man. But he knew he would get dirty and smeared with blood if he tried to clean up the poor fellow. So he also hurried off without helping.

"Two men supposed to be good and kind had selfishly gone on, rather than put themselves out by stopping to aid a stranger in need.

"More minutes dragged by, and the robbers' victim still lay unable to move. Then he heard the clip clop of hooves, as along came a donkey. On its back sat a Samaritan.

"Now Jews and Samaritans have never been the best of friends, so you would hardly expect a Samaritan to feel sorry for the Jew on the ground. But this man was different. He leapt off his donkey and knelt down beside the Jew, dabbing his wounds with something soothing, and bandaging the worst of his cuts.

"Then the Samaritan lifted the Jew on to his own donkey, and walked beside it until they came to an inn.

"Next day the Samaritan left, but first he paid the innkeeper to care for the Jew until he was better."

Jesus ended his story by asking, "Now which of these three was a true neighbour to the injured man?"

"The one who helped him," answered the expert in Bible law.

"Do as he did, then," said Jesus.

LUKE 10:25–37

"But a Samaritan who was going that way came upon him, and when he saw him he was moved to pity. He went up and bandaged his wounds, bathing them with oil and wine."
Luke 10:33

THE LOST SHEEP

The teachers and Pharisees were always grumbling about Jesus. Not only did he challenge their position of power and respectability, but he mixed with the wrong sort of people.

"This man welcomes outcasts and even has dinner with them," the Pharisees muttered when they saw Jesus talking with the tax collectors, fellow Jews who worked for the Roman occupying forces and often cheated people. So Jesus told the Pharisees and teachers stories to explain why he spent so much time with the people everyone else avoided.

"Imagine you are a shepherd and you have a hundred sheep to look after," he said. "One night you discover one of your flock is missing. What would you do? You would not think, 'Never mind, I have still got ninety-nine, I will forget about the other one.' No! You would leave those ninety-nine sheep safely grazing in the pasture and search high and low for that lost sheep. You would go on looking all night if need be. You would search behind rocks and under bushes, you would even look over steep cliffs to make sure it had not slipped down. You would carry on calling for it until eventually a weak bleating noise would tell you it was trapped in a bramble.

"Then you would lift the poor animal on your shoulders and take it back home. You would be so relieved that you had found the lost sheep that, when you got home, you would tell all your friends the good news and have a party to celebrate.

"It will be just like that in heaven when one person like these tax collectors turns his back on his crooked ways and looks to God to help him. There will be more celebration about one bad man turning to God than about ninety-nine respectable people who do not need to repent.

"Let me give you another example: a woman has ten silver coins. On losing one, would she not put all the lights on and sweep the floor thoroughly, and look in every nook and cranny until she finds it? And on finding the lost coin, she would call all her friends and neighbours together and ask them to celebrate with her. For the coin that was lost, is now found.

"In the same way, God will call the heavenly angels together and there will be great rejoicing over one sinner who repents, that is, one sinner who has found God again."

But Jesus could see that these stubborn Pharisees were still not fully convinced. So he went on to tell them the well-known parable of the Prodigal Son.

MATTHEW 18:12–14; LUKE 15:1–10

"Or again, if a woman has ten silver coins and loses one of them, does she not light the lamp, sweep out the house, and look in every corner till she finds it?"
Luke 15:8

"Suppose someone has a
hundred sheep, and one of
them strays, does he not
leave the other ninety-nine
on the hillside and go in
search of the one that
strayed?"
Matthew 18:12

THE PRODIGAL SON

"Let me tell you about a man who had two sons," said Jesus. "The younger of the two was reckless and impatient by nature. He knew that when his father died, he would be given half the family wealth. But he could not wait that long. 'Father,' he said one day, 'I want you to give me my part of the inheritance now.' His father agreed to this and gave him half his estate.

"The young man sold the estate off immediately, and with the money he set off to start a new, exciting life elsewhere.

"Everything was fine at first. He travelled to a foreign country and began to enjoy himself. But slowly his money began to run out.

"Soon he was alone, in a strange country, with no money and no friends. Sad and lonely he took the only work offered to him – looking after a herd of pigs on a scrubby hillside.

"One day, miserable and hungry, he sat staring at the pigs, wishing he could eat the bean pods they were busily chewing. His thoughts returned to home. He wished desperately that he had never left. Even the servants at home were better-off than he was now. They always had plenty to eat and were well looked after.

"Then he had an idea. 'I know,' he said to himself, 'I'll go home to my father, tell him I'm sorry, and ask for a job as a servant.' He left his pigs and set off.

"And so, one day his father was looking out from his house when he saw a small figure on the horizon. As it grew larger, his father's heart gave a jolt. Could it be? Surely not! But yes . . . It was his son. With a great shout of love and joy the father ran towards the dejected figure approaching him. With tears in his eyes he hugged and kissed him.

"'Father,' the son said, 'I have done wrong against God and against you. I don't deserve to be called your son any more . . .' But his father brushed the boy's apologies aside. 'Quick!' he called to his servants, 'Bring the best clothes in the house and put them on him. Bring a gold ring and shoes. Then get the best beef calf we have and roast it ready for a great feast. My son has come home! I never thought I would see him again. It is just as if he had returned from the dead.'

"So there was great happiness in the house and soon the feasting began, with dancing and singing and lots of laughter. But not everyone was so pleased. The elder brother, who had stayed at home, was on his way back from a hard day's work in the fields. He saw lights blazing in the house and heard the music and singing as it floated across the fields.

"Curious, he called one of the servants over. 'What's going on?' he asked. With a broad grin, the servant replied, 'It's your brother, sir! He's come back home and your father's killed the prize calf to celebrate!'

"Instead of being overjoyed, the older brother became angry. He refused to go into the house and stalked off in a rage. Hearing of this, his father left the party and came outside to try and persuade him to join the celebrations.

"'What have I got to celebrate?' the son grunted. 'Here I am, I've worked hard for you. I've never disobeyed your orders all these years and what do I get? Nothing! But my brother takes your money, goes off abroad and wastes it on parties and drink. When he comes back home with nothing, what do you do? You kill the prize calf for a celebration feast.'

"'Look,' said the father, 'You are always here, and I am glad of it. Everything I have is yours – you know that. But we have to celebrate and be happy. We all thought your brother was dead and gone, but here he is at home. He was lost and is found.'"

LUKE 15:11–32

"But while he was still a long way off his father saw him, and his heart went out to him; he ran to meet him, flung his arms round him, and kissed him."
Luke 15:20–21

THE PARABLE OF THE TALENTS

Some people rather liked the idea of following Jesus as he travelled from village to village. He was so popular with the people. But Jesus soon put them right. He told people that to follow him all the way was going to be hard. They would have to leave security behind them and take risks. He expected his followers to do more than just listen. It was no use, he said, just believing in his power and doing nothing about it. One day they would have to account for their actions. Jesus told his disciples a story to show what he meant.

"Once there was a man who was setting off on a long journey. He was wealthy, with money to spare and he wanted his servants to make valuable use of their time while he was away. So, bearing in mind the varying degrees of ability of each of his three servants, he gave them control over certain amounts of money. To one he gave five thousand silver coins amounting to five talents. To the second servant he gave two thousand similar coins and to the third, one thousand. Then, leaving them in charge of his property, he left on his journey.

"The first servant counted the five thousand coins carefully. He knew that if he used the money wisely, he could make even more for his master. So thinking to himself, 'I'll make this money work,' he invested it.

"The second servant with his smaller amount decided to use the money to earn more for his master. But the third servant did not know what to do. It was risky, he thought, trying to use the money to get more. What if he failed? In the end he thought that the safest way was to wrap the money up and bury it.

"After some months, the master returned home. He summoned his men to see how they had done.

"The first servant handed over the five thousand coins he had been given. Then he said, 'Here is another five thousand I earned with the first sum.' The master was delighted. 'Well done,' he said. 'You have proved yourself with small amounts, so I shall promote you and give you responsibility over a great

deal more. You will be rewarded for your efforts.'

"Then the second servant gave his master two thousand coins back and added another two thousand he had managed to earn. 'You have done well with so little,' the master said. 'Because you have shown yourself capable, I shall promote you too. You will be rewarded and given more responsibility.'

"The master then turned to the third servant to whom he had given one thousand coins. The servant approached sheepishly. 'Well?' said the master.

'Master,' he replied, 'I know you are a hard man and I was afraid that I would make a mistake and so I didn't do anything. I just hid the money until you came back. Look,' he said, unwrapping the bag of coins, 'It's still here.'

"The master was angry. 'You did not even put it in a bank where it would have been safe and would have still earned a bit of interest. Give that money to the servant who earned five thousand. You do not deserve it. Reward goes to those people who have worked hard and shown initiative. Those who make no effort will have even what they have been given taken away from them.'"

MATTHEW 25:14–30; LUKE 19:12–27

The Wise and Foolish Maidens

Jesus knew that time was short. When his life and work on earth were finished he would go back to be with his Father in heaven. But he also knew that one day he would come back for those who believed in him. He wanted his followers to be alert – to live as if they were always ready for his return. It was foolish not to, he said to his disciples, and he told them this story:

"Once there were ten girls who had been asked to take part in a wedding procession. They were to escort the bridegroom to his wedding where the wedding feast was due to take place. Each of them had an oil lamp which they would use to light the procession. They were very excited because weddings were grand festive occasions and the lamp-lit procession through the night was one of the best parts.

"Five of them knew what they were supposed to do and brought extra oil to make sure their lamps did not give out half way through. The other five did not think at all. They brought their lamps but no extra oil with them.

"As it happened, the bridegroom was late and they had to wait for him, using up valuable oil as they sat around. Then one by one they began to nod off to sleep, until just after midnight, when the cry rang out, 'The bridegroom is here!'

"That was when the trouble started. The ten girls prepared their lamps for the procession. The five girls who had thought about what they were doing, put in the extra oil. The others, to their horror, saw that their lamps were dimming.

"'Quick,' they shouted to the other five, 'give us some of your oil, or our lamps will go out!'

"'We can't,' said the other girls. 'We have only just

enough for ourselves. You will have to buy some. But hurry.'

"So the foolish girls rushed off to buy more oil. While they were away, the bridegroom arrived. 'Right, let's go then,' he said. The glittering procession wound its way to the house where the wedding feast was being held. Everyone trooped inside and the door was bolted behind them.

"Some while later, the other five girls arrived, breathless. 'We are here. Let us in!' they shouted.

"'Certainly not!' came the reply from inside the house, 'I don't know who you are. You are not invited to this wedding. Go away!' So they were left furious with themselves, because they had not been ready for the big occasion.

"Remember, do not be like those five foolish girls. Be on your guard," said Jesus.

Jesus told the Pharisees that they were sometimes foolish too, but in a different way. They had studied the Old Testament and so ought to know how God wanted them to live, but they did not.

"It is like a blind man leading another blind man," said Jesus. "They will get nowhere. In the end, both men will end up falling into a ditch because neither can see the way. You Pharisees are like a person who keeps on fussing because someone has a speck of dust in his eye, completely ignoring the fact that he has a great log in his own! You cannot even see to take out the speck, because of the log in your own eye. Get rid of the log first, then worry about other people.

"The Pharisees do not practise what they preach," Jesus said to the crowds. "They load restrictions on people but do nothing to help them."

Turning to the Pharisees, Jesus said, "You blind guides, you give God a tenth of every single thing, down to the herbs you cook with, but you neglect the really important teachings, such as justice and mercy and honesty. You would strain a gnat out of your drink and then swallow a camel! And you are so careful to clean the outside of your cups and plates while the rich food you eat and drink from them you have obtained by being ruthlessly selfish."

MATTHEW 7:1–6; 15:10–20; 25:1–13; MARK 7:14–23; LUKE 6:37–42

THE SHEEP AND THE GOATS

When Jesus referred to himself, he sometimes used the phrase 'Son of Man'. One day he told an astonishing story.

"When the Son of Man comes as King with a mighty force of angels," Jesus said, "he will set up his royal throne. Before him will be gathered the nations of the world in all their millions. Then, just like a shepherd separating the sheep from the goats when they have all been grazing together, he will divide the people into two groups. He will put the sheep on the right hand and the goats on the left.

"Then, looking at the people on the right, he will say, 'Come, you have been blessed by my Father. You can now take your place in God's Kingdom which has been prepared for you ever since the world was created. I was hungry and you fed me; I was thirsty and you gave me something to drink; I was a stranger and you welcomed me into your homes; I was naked and you gave me clothes to wear; I was ill and you nursed me back to health; I was in prison and you visited me.'

"Then those people judged to be righteous will look puzzled and ask the King, 'When was this Lord? When did we see you hungry, thirsty, lonely, naked, ill or in prison?' The King will reply, 'Whenever you did these things for the least person, you did it for me.'

"Having said this, the Son of Man will turn to the group he placed on his left and say, 'You must leave here. You are under God's curse and deserve the eternal fire prepared for the Devil and his angels. I was hungry, but you would not feed me; I was thirsty and you refused me any drink; I was a stranger but you did not show me any hospitality; I was naked but I got no clothes from you, I was in prison and I was ill, but you did not lift a finger to help me.'

"But the people on the King's left will look astonished and protest. 'But Lord, when did we see you in trouble like this? If we had known it was you, naturally we would have helped.' The King will reply, 'Let me tell you this. Whenever you refused help to anyone in need, you refused to help me!' The King will send them to eternal punishment. But the righteous will go to eternal life."

In another story about judgement, Jesus made it equally clear who he was.

"Once there was an owner of a vineyard. He needed to make a long journey abroad, so he decided to let out his large estate to tenants. It was a new estate with everything that a tenant farmer could need. The owner found tenants and drew up an agreement about a share of the produce as rent. Then he set out, leaving the tenants in control.

"When the first harvest time came round, the tenants gathered in all the grapes. As agreed, a servant of the owner came to collect a share of the harvest. But the tenants refused to part with any of the produce, beat up the servant and sent him packing. The owner sent another servant, but the tenants beat him before running him off the land. The owner sent a third servant. The tenants murdered him.

"This went on until the owner had no one else to send. No one except his son. 'Surely, they will respect my son,' said the owner to himself. Reluctantly he sent his son off to the vineyards.

"But the tenants could not care less that this was the owner's son. In fact, their immediate reaction was, 'Look, this is the owner's son. If we get rid of him the property will be ours.' So they seized the son, killed him and threw his body out into the yard.

"What should the owner do?" asked Jesus. "Come and kill those men who murdered his son and give the vineyard to new tenants. You have read the scriptures where it says, 'The stone which the builders threw out because it was no use, turned out to be the foundation stone of the new building.' That is what God has done."

MATTHEW *21*:33–46, *25*:31–46; MARK *12*:1–11; LUKE *20*:9–18

180

THE WORKERS IN THE VINEYARD

Jesus told another story about an owner of a vineyard to show what God's way is like.

"The owner of a vineyard went out at sunrise to the market square to hire men to work in his vineyard. He settled with them what they should earn for the day's work. Then three hours later he went to the market square again and hired more men. He told them he would pay a proper wage. At noon he was still short of hands, so he hired yet more men.

"At about five o'clock, the owner went to the square and saw men hanging about. 'Why aren't you working?' he asked. 'Because no one has taken us on,' they said. 'Then you can go to my vineyard and pick grapes,' the owner said.

"When night fell, the owner called the workmen and paid them each the same amount of money, starting with those who had begun work at five o'clock.

"Some of the men began grumbling at the vineyard owner. 'These fellows who started late have only done an hour's work and you have treated them exactly the same as us. And we have had to work through the heat of the day.'

"The vineyard owner replied: 'I am not treating you badly. We agreed on what you would be paid. Take your money and go. I want to give these latecomers as much as you. Can't I use my own money as I want? Or does my generosity make you jealous?'"

Another time Jesus told a story aimed at the rich

"These latecomers did only one hour's work, yet we have sweated the whole day long in the blazing sun!"
Matthew 20:12

and self-satisfied. "Make sure you do not get greedy," Jesus warned. "A person's life is not only what he owns, no matter how rich he might be."

"There was once a rich farmer. He had a great deal of fertile land and it bore good crops. One day it occurred to him that he was producing more than he could store. He began to make plans. 'I will demolish the barns I have at the moment and build much bigger ones. Then I can sit back. I shall have everything I need for years. I can take life easy and generally enjoy myself.'

"But God said to him, 'You fool! You are going to die tonight. Your life will be gone. Now who will get all those things you have selfishly kept to yourself?'" Jesus ended the story by saying, "Some people who appear wealthy, are not rich in God's sight."

MATTHEW 20:1–16; LUKE 12:13–21

JESUS MEETS NICODEMUS

One night a man called Nicodemus came to see Jesus. He was an important man in Jewish affairs. He was a Pharisee, a member of the Sanhedrin, and a well-respected religious teacher. Nicodemus had heard much about Jesus. He wanted to find out more about his teachings.

But Nicodemus was not very brave about going to see him. Jesus was being watched by the Jewish leaders as a possible trouble-maker. Nicodemus was afraid to be seen talking to him. It would not be good for his career.

So, under cover of darkness, Nicodemus made his way to where Jesus was staying in Jerusalem. "Master," he began, "we know God has sent you to teach us. No one could do such miracles unless God were with him."

Jesus knew well that Nicodemus only half-understood what he had come to do. He said: "Believe me, Nicodemus, it is not possible for you to understand about being part of God's Kingdom, unless you are born again."

This baffled Nicodemus. "What on earth do you mean?" he asked. "How can an old man like me go back inside his mother and be born again like a baby?"

Patiently, Jesus replied, "It just happens. I'm telling you the truth. Men and women can only produce human life. The Holy Spirit can give people new life from heaven. Don't be surprised at me saying everyone has to be born again. Take the wind as an example. It blows wherever it likes. You can hear it, but you can't see where it comes from, or where it is going. In the same way, you can't explain how the Spirit brings new life to a person."

"I still don't understand it," said Nicodemus. Jesus smiled as he looked at him. "You are thought a great teacher," Jesus said gently, "Yet you can't begin to understand what I am talking about? I assure you I'm telling the truth. This is the most important thing I have come to say, yet somehow you cannot understand. If I tell you about things which are happening around you all the time, and you don't believe me, how will you understand if I begin to tell you about heaven?

"Only the Son of Man," Jesus went on, referring to himself, "has ever seen heaven, because that was where he came from." Jesus continued as if he were telling a story about someone else. He explained how 'the Son of Man' was going to die, and be lifted up so that everyone could see him.

Jesus told Nicodemus why God had sent him to earth. "God loved this world so much that he sent his only Son, so that anyone who believes in him should not be lost, but have new life. He did not send him to judge the world, but to save it, and anyone who honestly believes in him, will enjoy this new life."

Nicodemus thought a great deal about what Jesus had told him. The truth of what Jesus had said affected him deeply; he never forgot it. Much later, Nicodemus became one of Jesus' followers. He had found the courage to follow him openly.

JOHN 3:1–21

"The wind blows where it wills; you hear the sound of it, but you do not know where it comes from or where it is going. So it is with everyone who is born from the Spirit!"
John 3:8

Signs of the End of the World

As Jesus and his disciples were leaving the Temple one day, they called his attention to the building itself.

"Just look at those stones," they said, "aren't they magnificent?" Jesus looked where they were pointing and said, "The time will come when not one stone is left on top of another. The whole place will be in ruins."

"When will this be?" his disciples asked in astonishment. "And what signs will there be to show that it is about to happen?" Jesus began to tell them about the future, foretelling the destruction of Jerusalem (which actually took place in AD 70). Then he went on to say that one day the world itself would come to an end. Then Jesus would return to take his own people to be with him in heaven.

"Be on your guard," he told them. "When I have left you, many will come claiming to speak for me. 'I am the Messiah,' they will say, and people will believe them. There will be wars close by and news of yet more, but do not be disturbed. These things have to happen, but they do not mean that the end has come. There will be famines and earthquakes everywhere. You yourselves will be arrested, put in prison and some of you will be put to death for your belief. All mankind will hate you because of me. Some people will lose their faith but those who hold out to the end will be saved. The good news of the Kingdom of God will be preached throughout the whole world – only then will the end come."

The signs of the final end, Jesus warned them, could not be read easily. Absolutely no one would know for sure when Jesus would return.

"Let the fig tree teach you a lesson," Jesus said. "When it has put out green shoots and its leaves begin to sprout, you know that summer is near. In just the same way, when you see the signs you will know the time is near. But mark my words. No one will know when the hour or even the day has arrived. The coming of the Son of Man will be exactly as it was in Noah's time – life went on as normal, right up to the very day when Noah went into the boat. It will be the same at my coming. Two men will be working in a field. One will be taken away, the other left behind. Two women will be doing their daily chores. One will be taken, the other left. So be on your guard! The Son of Man will come when you are least expecting him.

w francis phillips.

"But there will be no mistaking when the Son of Man comes. It will be like the lightning which flashes across the whole sky, lighting it up in a blaze of glory from east to west. The sky will grow dark, the moon will stop shining, the stars will fall from the sky and the powers holding the planets on course will go out of control. Then the sign of the Son of Man will appear in the sky. The population of all the world will weep as they see the Son of Man riding on the clouds of heaven as he comes in mighty glory. A great trumpet will sound a fanfare and God's angels will go throughout the world gathering together his chosen people from one end of the Earth to the other."

At another time Jesus talked about his return for his people as a harvest. He said. "The coming of the Kingdom will happen like this. A farmer sows seed in his field. Then while he goes about his work, day after day, the seeds sprout and grow. First the young stalks appear, then the ear, and then the seeds swell in the ear. Then one day the farmer sees that the corn is ripe. He gets out his sickle and begins to cut and gather it in. The harvest has come."

Jesus' words seemed solemn, even gloomy warnings, but he knew that it was vital that people should leave their wrong doing, believe whole heartedly in him and be ready for his return.

MATTHEW 24; MARK 13; LUKE 21:5–38

LAZARUS IS RAISED FROM THE DEAD

One of the many wonderful stories about Jesus tells how he brought a dead man back to life.

The story begins with bad news from the little town of Bethany. Martha and her sister Mary, who both knew Jesus, sent him a message: "Lazarus, your friend and our brother, is very ill."

You might think Jesus would have hurried over to help. But fond as he was of Lazarus, he waited another two days. His reason will become plain in a moment.

At last he told his disciples he was ready to go. This worried them.

They said, "Only a few days back the Jewish leaders in that part of Palestine were trying to kill you."

Jesus seemed quite unconcerned for his safety. He said, "Lazarus is dead. I am glad I was not there when it happened – going now will give you fresh reasons for believing in me." So reluctantly they set out with Jesus for Bethany.

On the way they met Martha. Brushing tears from her eyes, she sobbed, "Lord, if you had been here he would still be alive."

But Jesus calmly told her, "Your brother will live again, for I bring the dead to life. Anyone who believes in me will live again – for ever. Do you believe me Martha?"

"Yes, Lord, I do," she said. "I believe you are the Son of God, the Messiah that we have waited for."

Jesus stayed outside the village while Martha went home to fetch Mary. She returned with a group of Jewish leaders who had been consoling her. Seeing them all wailing and crying brought tears of pity to Jesus' eyes.

One Jewish leader murmured, "See how fond he was of Lazarus." But another said, "He made a blind man see – why didn't he save his own friend?"

Jesus asked where Lazarus was buried. Sadly they led him to the tomb where the dead man lay. It was a cave, closed by a huge stone.

"Roll the stone away," Jesus ordered. The people wondered what Jesus was going to do. After all, Lazarus had been dead four days.

Jesus spoke a short prayer. Then he cried, "Lazarus, come out!"

Something moved inside the darkness. Everyone shrank back with fright as a strange figure stepped out. It was a man, wrapped tightly in grave cloths from head to foot.

"Unbind him," Jesus commanded. Then everyone saw it was indeed Lazarus, back from the dead!

Many of the watching Jews now believed in Jesus' amazing powers. But the Jewish priests were afraid and jealous. They began to plan how to get rid of Jesus.

JOHN 11:1–44

Then he raised his voice in a great cry: "Lazarus, come out." The dead man came out, his hands and feet bound with linen bandages, his face wrapped in a cloth. Jesus said, "Loose him; let him go." John II:43–44

JESUS ENTERS JERUSALEM

One spring day Jesus set out on his last great journey – a trip to celebrate the yearly Passover feast in the Jewish capital, Jerusalem. By now he was famous; thousands adored him. But some Jewish priests in the city wanted him silenced. He knew his journey was risky, but he felt he must go.

When Jesus neared Jerusalem he sent two disciples to a small village, saying, "Bring me the young donkey that you'll find tied up there. Say your master must borrow it and will bring it back soon."

They duly returned with the animal, and threw their cloaks on its back as a makeshift saddle.

Then Jesus mounted the donkey and rode slowly up the steep, narrow road leading into the city.

Meanwhile, news of his coming had spread. A huge crowd collected, and a great shout went up when the citizens saw Jesus approaching. People dashed into the road, dropping their coats for his donkey to walk on. Others strewed his path with a carpet of leafy palm branches.

All around him people were shouting, "Hail to the king! Blessed is he who comes in the Lord's name! Praise God for bringing back our father David's kingdom!"

It was a welcome fit for an emperor, for thousands believed that Jesus was not just a great religious teacher. They thought he was a new, powerful leader come to throw out their hated Roman rulers.

MATTHEW 21:1–11; MARK 11:1–10; LUKE 19:28–40; JOHN 12:12–19

THE LAST SUPPER

Although Jesus had many friends and followers, he had also made enemies, particularly among the chief priests and elders of the people, and they plotted to get rid of Jesus. They wanted to have him arrested, but did not want this to happen during the Passover celebrations, as they were frightened it would cause an uproar among the people.

Then Judas, one of Jesus' disciples, went to visit the chief priests, and offered to betray Jesus and hand him over to them. The chief priests were delighted and offered him thirty pieces of silver. From then on Judas looked out for an opportunity for betraying Jesus.

On the first evening of the Passover feast, Jesus planned where he and his disciples would eat. He said to two of them: "Go on ahead. Follow a man with a water pot to a house. Tell the person in charge you have come to see the room he has ready for us. He'll lead you upstairs to a large room set out for supper."

The disciples found things just as Jesus had said they would.

That evening, Jesus and his twelve disciples sat down to eat. "I have looked forward to eating this Passover meal with you." Jesus said. "The time of my death now approaches."

Then Jesus got up, took off his robe and tied a towel around his waist. He poured water into a basin and started to wash the disciples' feet and then he dried them with the towel. When it was Peter's turn, the disciple cried: "Surely you do not intend to wash my feet Lord!'

"You do not understand now, but you will, Peter." Jesus replied gently.

When Jesus had finished, he put his robe back on, and returned to the table.

Jesus solemnly studied their faces. He did not want to hurt them, but he had something important to say.

Sadly he announced, "One of you will betray me."

There was a shocked silence. Most of them could not believe it. But they knew Jesus had great insight into people's hearts. So one by one they asked, "Is it me?"

Jesus said nothing. Then a disciple called John, who was sitting near to Jesus, asked outright, "Who is it, Lord?" Jesus replied, "It is the one to whom I give bread dipped in sauce," and he gave the bread to

Simon Iscariot's son, Judas.

Jesus went on, "I have to die, just as the prophets foretold long ago." He knew that giving his life was the sacrifice that would bring people closer to God.

Jesus thanked God for the bread and the wine. He took the bread and broke it, then he handed the bread and wine to his disciples, saying, "Eat – this is my body. Drink – this is my blood."

He told them that when he was no longer with them they must eat bread and drink wine in his memory. It was a meal none of them ever forgot.

MATTHEW *26*:17–29; MARK *14*:12–25; LUKE *22*:7–30; JOHN *13*:1–30

During supper he took bread, and having said the blessing he broke it and gave it to them, with the words: "Take this; this is my body." Then he took a cup, and having offered thanks to God he gave it to them; and they all drank from it. And he said to them, "This is my blood, the blood of the covenant, shed for many."
Mark 14:22–24

THE GARDEN OF GETHSEMANE

All seemed peaceful that night as Jesus and his disciples left the supper room in Jerusalem, and walked towards their lodgings. But Jesus knew that his enemies were close and ready to strike.

Jesus told his disciples they would soon desert him. But Peter cried out angrily, "I'll never leave you!"

Jesus smiled and said, "Peter, three times tonight before the cock crows you will say you don't even know me."

They came to an old olive grove, and Jesus told his disciples to rest while he walked off alone to pray. It was quiet and beautiful there in the garden of Gethsemane, and moonlight shone through the trees.

Jesus felt suddenly terribly afraid when he thought of the tortures and death in store for him. He went on a little further, then threw himself down on the ground and prayed that God might let him escape all this pain. Yet in his heart he knew that his death was part of a plan to bring people nearer to God. Looking up to heaven, he cried out to God, "Let your will be done!"

Meanwhile, his tired disciples had fallen asleep. All was silent. Suddenly there came a loud tramping of feet and a flashing of lights. The disciples awoke with a start to see Judas leading a crowd of priests and soldiers into the olive grove, and straight towards Jesus.

Judas embraced Jesus as though they were still friends. But Jesus knew that this was an act of betrayal. Judas' embrace was really a signal, showing the soldiers which man to seize and arrest.

At first, Jesus' disciples tried to put up a fight. Peter grabbed his sword and attacked the men who were arresting Jesus. He cut off an ear from the head of the high priest's servant. But Jesus did not want the servant to suffer, so he healed the cut immediately.

Jesus did not offer any resistance himself. When his disciples saw it was hopeless they ran away, just as Jesus had told them they would.

As Jesus was marched off to the home of the high priest, only Peter dared to follow. Although he could not go inside with Jesus, Peter waited about in the courtyard to see what would happen. He was frightened for himself as well as for Jesus.

A servant girl noticed him and cried: "I know you. You were with Jesus!" Peter at once denied it in front of everyone.

He wandered out through the gateway of the courtyard, and another servant saw him and said: "You are a friend of Jesus." But Peter answered: "I don't know him."

Then some people who were standing nearby cried: "Yes, you are one of Jesus' followers, you are from Galilee, aren't you?"

At this Peter cried out: "Look, I don't even know who you're talking about!" At that moment a cock crowed. Peter then remembered that Jesus had said he would deny him three times, and he wept with sorrow.

Only days earlier, Jerusalem had welcomed Jesus as a king. Now many of the city's leaders treated him as if he were a criminal.

MATTHEW 26:30–58, 69–75; MARK 14:26–54, 66–72; LUKE 22:39–62; JOHN 18:1–11, 15–18, 25–27

Going straight up to Jesus, he said, "Hail, Rabbi!" and kissed him. Jesus replied, "Friend, do what you are here to do." Then they came forward, seized Jesus and held him fast.
Matthew 26:49–50

THE CRUCIFIXION

In the high priest's house, Jesus was questioned closely about his teachings. Jesus said, "I have taught openly in the synagogue and in the Temple, why don't you ask those who heard me?"

At this one of the attendants struck Jesus across the face. "Is that the way to speak to the high priest?" he demanded.

"If I was wrong, tell me in what way; if I am right, why do you hit me?" replied Jesus.

The high priest then asked Jesus directly, "Are you the Messiah, the Son of God?"

"I am," said Jesus.

At this the high priest tore his clothes in anger. "Blasphemy!" he cried.

It was agreed that Jesus was guilty and should be put to death. But the Romans were the rulers, and only they could execute Jesus. So the next morning, Jesus was taken by the chief priests, elders and scribes to see Pilate, the Roman governor.

"This man claims to be a king," they said.

Pilate looked at Jesus and said, "Well, *are* you the king of the Jews?" Jesus answered quietly, "Those are your words."

The chief priests continued their charges against Jesus, but to Pilate's astonishment, Jesus remained calm and silent throughout.

At last, Pilate became exasperated and said, "Look, I can see no fault in this man."

Now it was the custom during the feast of the Passover that one prisoner should be allowed to go free. Pilate took Jesus before the waiting crowd and offered to free him. But the crowd chanted, "Not Jesus, free Barabbas, free Barabbas!" The chief priests and elders had spoken to the crowd earlier and had persuaded them to ask for the release of Barabbas, who was a nationalist and a man of violence.

"What do you want me to do with Jesus, then?" cried Pilate.

"Crucify him! Crucify him!" yelled the crowd.

Pilate saw that there was nothing else he could do, and the crowd looked in danger of starting a riot. He ordered that Jesus be flogged and then hung from a wooden cross until he died. This was a common way of executing criminals.

The government's soldiers took Jesus away and began mocking and taunting him. They took off his clothes and made him wear a scarlet cloak, then they took some thorny branches and bent them into the shape of a crown and put this on his head. They placed a stick in his right hand, then they bowed down before him and laughed at him saying, "Hail, king of the Jews!" Jesus was then led away to be crucified.

Jesus was forced to walk out to the hill of execution carrying the heavy cross on his back, though a stranger called Simon of Cyrene helped him. Then men nailed his wrists to the wooden arms of the cross, and raised it upright. Above Jesus' head someone fastened a sign that read: *The King of the Jews.*

For hours, Jesus hung on the cross tormented by his enemies.

"Look at you now!" they jeered. "If you're who you say, why don't you save yourself and come down?"

Jesus' pain-filled gaze wandered over the crowd who had come to watch. Suddenly he noticed his mother Mary. She was standing near Jesus' disciple John, and crying. Jesus told John to take her home and be like a son to her.

As Jesus grew weaker the sky darkened and the ground trembled. Men who had jeered grew afraid that he really had been God's son, and this was God's way of showing his anger at what they had done.

Suddenly Jesus cried out, "Father, I give my spirit into your care! It is finished." Then he died.

MATTHEW 26:57–68; 27:1–2, 11–50; MARK 14:55–65; 15:1–37; LUKE 22:63–71; 23:1–46; JOHN 18:12–40; 19:1–30

THE RESURRECTION

Perhaps the most astonishing of all biblical tales are those about what happened after Jesus died.

No one doubted he had died – a soldier made sure of it by jabbing a spear in Jesus' side as he hung on the cross. That night, friends secretly took his body, wrapped it in a scented cloth and laid it in a tomb, shut by a huge stone.

Then, on Sunday morning, two days later, extraordinary things began to happen.

When Jesus' follower Mary Magdalene visited the tomb, she found to her surprise that the door lay open. She was horrified to find no corpse inside. Mary wept to think that anyone should steal her teacher's body. Then, through her tears, she glimpsed two angels sitting in the tomb where Jesus had been lying.

Just then she heard a voice and turned to see a man behind her.

"Why do you cry?" he asked. "Who are you looking for?"

Blinking at him through her tears, she thought she saw a gardener.

"If you have taken him away," she sobbed, "please tell me where he is."

The man just said, "Mary!" and suddenly she knew it was Jesus – the dead Jesus, but standing there as much alive as she was! Imagine her amazement and delight.

Mary Magdalene was only the first to see Jesus rise from the dead. That night, the Bible says, he appeared to his disciples as they met secretly behind locked doors. It was as if he walked through the wall, as ghosts are said to do. One disciple, Thomas, was not there on this occasion, and he doubted when he heard the story whether the real Jesus had been there at all.

The next time Jesus appeared, he proved he was real by making Thomas feel the scars left by the crucifixion – scars where nails had pierced his wrists and where the soldier's spear had left a gash in his side. "You believe now," said Jesus, "but blessed indeed are those who have not seen me, yet still believe."

Jesus appeared to his disciples at least once more. But things were never quite as they had been before he died. Now he never stayed for long, and sometimes they did not even recognize him at first.

It was like this when seven of them had been fishing on the Sea of Galilee. They had rowed around all night throwing out their nets, without landing a single fish.

As dawn broke a man standing on the beach called out, "Any luck?"

"No!" they shouted back.

Then he cried, "Throw the net on the right-hand side of the boat. You'll find plenty there."

They did – and he was right! When they hauled the net ashore, scores of big, juicy fishes were flopping helplessly inside.

John knew this was not simply luck. Realizing who the man must be, he shouted, "It's the Lord!"

Jesus stayed for breakfast. His last message to his followers was this: "Go out into the world and tell everyone the good news that I bring. Those who believe, and are baptized, will be saved."

Jesus' work on earth was over, and the Bible says that when he finished speaking, his disciples saw him taken up into heaven.

Now it was up to them to carry on the task he had begun.

MATTHEW 27:57–60; 28:1–10, 16–20; MARK 15:46–47; 16; LUKE 23:50–56; 24; JOHN 19:38–42 TO 21

Then he said to Thomas, "Reach your finger here; look at my hands. Reach your hand here and put it into my side. Be unbelieving no longer, but believe." John 20:27–29

Jesus said, "Come and have breakfast." None of the disciples dared to ask "Who are you?" They knew it was the Lord.
John 21:12

THE STONING OF STEPHEN

Jesus used to warn his followers that enemies would beat and torture them for what they preached. He said that some of them would even die because of their beliefs.

People who perish in that way are known as martyrs. Since Jesus Christ himself hung on a cross about two thousand years ago, thousands of his followers have met a martyr's death. The first of them was a young Jew called Stephen.

Stephen has earned a special place among Jerusalem's early Christians (as Christ's followers became known). For he was not just deeply religious; he was clever too. Christian leaders made Stephen one of seven deacons, with the job of caring for the Christian poor.

But Stephen became best known for preaching powerful sermons, and for cleverly defending his Christian faith in arguments.

One day, a group of Jewish leaders tried to prove to Stephen that he was wrong when he preached that Jesus was the Son of God. But Stephen's answers were so wise that his opponents found they had no arguments left.

So, instead, they plotted to have him put to death.

First, they paid some men to tell lies about Stephen. This made people hate him, and led the Jewish leaders to arrest him and have him brought before their council. As Stephen faced his judges and accusers he guessed how horribly his trial would end. But he listened calmly as lying witnesses accused him of cursing God and Moses. Any Jew found guilty of such charges was likely to be sentenced to death.

The judges watched Stephen closely to see how he reacted. To their surprise, instead of looking angry or ashamed, his face seemed to glow with glory like an angel's.

The high priest was so astonished that he felt Stephen deserved at least a chance to defend himself. So he asked, "Did you really say these things?"

The Jewish leader soon wished he had not invited Stephen to speak, for once he began he seemed to talk for hours. Stephen reminded everyone of the history of the Jews from the time of Abraham onwards. Then he told how, one after another, rulers had ignored God's voice and killed his prophets.

Stephen finished by saying, "You are just as bad as they were, for you killed Jesus – God's Saviour sent to earth to help mankind.

Stephen, full of grace and power, began to do great wonders and signs among the people. Some members of the synagogue called the Synagogue of Freedmen, comprising Cyrenians and Alexandrians and people from Cilicia and Asia, came forward and argued with Stephen, but could not hold their own against the inspired wisdom with which he spoke.
Acts 6:8–10

But Stephen, filled with the Holy Spirit, and gazing intently up to heaven, saw the glory of God, and Jesus standing at God's right hand. "Look!" he said. "I see the heavens opened and the Son of Man standing at the right hand of God."
Acts 7:55–56

The longer Stephen talked, the more angry the Jewish leaders became.

At the end he could almost hear them grind their teeth with rage. Stephen knew they felt furious because he had shown *they* were the truly guilty ones. He also knew nothing he could say would affect the court's verdict.

Yet this knowledge only made him braver. Gazing up into the sky he said, "I see Jesus standing next to God in heaven."

It was the last straw. Until then Stephen's enemies had kept fairly quiet. Now they shouted him down, and clapped their hands over their ears to shut out the sound of Stephen's voice.

In fact there was no verdict. The court became a mob that dragged him out, rushed him through narrow streets, past the city gate, and down a stony track.

Stephen knew his end was near as the mob left him standing alone, while they began to search the ground for chunks of rock.

Moments later they began to hurl stones at Stephen's defenceless body. Stephen was soon knocked down. Bruised and bleeding, he still found strength to cry out, "Lord, forgive them!"

Stephen remembered, in his own agony, that Jesus had said this very prayer for those who had nailed him to the cross.

Soon afterwards Stephen was knocked unconscious, and died.

ACTS **6**:8–15; **7**

As they stoned him Stephen called out, "Lord Jesus, receive my spirit." He fell on his knees and cried aloud, "Lord do not hold this sin against them," and with that he died.
Acts 7:59–60

ON THE ROAD TO DAMASCUS

No one hated Christians more bitterly than a young man called Saul. Yet one day Saul would want to make the whole world believe in Jesus' Christian teachings. This story from the Bible tells how he changed his mind.

Young Saul believed that all the Christians were wicked, because they claimed that their leader, Jesus, was the Son of God. Saul felt this must be untrue, and anyone who said it deserved the very harshest of punishments for such a terrible lie.

In fact, Saul gladly looked after the heavy cloaks thrown off by other Jews, when they stoned the first Christian martyr, Stephen, to death.

Later on, Saul did his best to crush all the Christians in Jerusalem. He rushed from house to house, hauling Christian men and women off to jail and execution. Hundreds of Christians fled from the city, but Saul was determined to track them down. So, when he heard that some of them had travelled to Damascus, he set off with troops to drag them back in chains.

Saul didn't guess that this trip would change his life for ever.

After a long, hot journey over mountains and dusty deserts, Saul had almost reached Damascus. He paused on a hilltop, and gazed down at the plain before him. After all that rock and dust it was pleasant to see green fields, olive groves and vineyards. And there, shimmering in the sunlight, rose the walls and towers of the lovely city.

But Saul's smile turned to a frown, as he remembered that his task was catching Christians.

Just then, the bright sunlight seemed to grow still brighter. In a moment the travellers found themselves bathed in a flash of light so dazzling that it almost seemed to burn through their eyes.

Saul glanced up – and fell back, blinded. As he lay on the ground bewildered, he heard a strange voice. It was not one of his companions speaking, and the voice seemed to echo in his head. It said. "Saul, Saul, why do you persecute me?"

Saul realized the voice must come from God. "Who are you, Lord?" he asked.

"I am Jesus," came the answer.

Then the voice continued, "Go into the city, and you will be told what to do." At once, Saul felt that the Christians were right and he had been wrong; Jesus *was* the Son of God.

The light faded, the voice disappeared, and Saul struggled to his feet. His companions saw that he had lost his sight and so they led him to Damascus. Here he lay for three days without food or drink. He thought of the voice he had heard, and he seemed to hear it again, telling him that a Christian would come and heal his eyes.

Meanwhile, news of Saul's arrival had reached the Christians of Damascus, and they were terrified. But one of them, called Ananias, had a strange dream. Jesus came to him and told him to help Saul. So, although Ananias knew only too well what Saul could do to him, he went to where Saul was staying.

"Jesus has sent me to you," said Ananias. "He wants you to be a Christian." And he laid his hands gently on Saul's eyes. Immediately, Saul could see again! Minutes later, Saul was baptized.

From then on Saul was a different man. He made friends with the people he had once hated, and he preached Christian ideas in the Jewish temples. Everyone who heard him was astounded. "Isn't this the man who used to try to destroy the Christians?" they asked.

ACTS *9*:1–22

There was in Damascus a disciple named Ananias. He had a vision in which he heard the Lord say: "Ananias!" "Here I am, Lord," he answered. The Lord said to him, "Go to Straight Street, to the house of Judas, and ask for a man from Tarsus named Saul. You will find him at prayer;" Acts 9:10–11

While he was still on the road and nearing Damascus, suddenly a light from the sky flashed all around him. He fell to the ground and heard a voice saying, "Saul, Saul, why are you persecuting me?"
Acts 9:3–4

Paul's Travels

Paul – as Saul was later called – became a great traveller, and he took Christian teachings to lands far beyond Palestine. In those days long-distance travel could be risky, and Paul was ship-wrecked three times.

Perhaps his most dangerous voyage was his last and longest. This was to the west, to Italy. As a Roman citizen Paul went to stand trial in Rome, wrongly accused of making trouble elsewhere in the Roman Empire.

Paul and three hundred others set sail from Egypt in a big, square-sailed grain ship. At first all went smoothly. Then an autumn gale sprang up and the ship began drifting helplessly through mountainous waves.

Passengers and crew began to panic. Then, above the roar of the storm, they heard Paul call out calmly, "Take courage! An angel of God has told me that we shall all be saved. Only the ship will be lost."

That helped to quieten them. But day after day the storm still drove them before it. Everyone was too scared to eat properly, until Paul set them an example.

At last the water grew shallow, and a sandy shore

loomed up through the spray. The crew raised the mainsail and the ship raced for the beach. But soon it ran aground, and began breaking up.

Soldiers, prisoners, merchants, crew – everyone had to swim for their lives. But just as Paul promised, all landed safely on what turned out to be the island of Malta.

Paul was now frail, old and soon to die. But he had achieved his life's work – the task of spreading Jesus' message far and wide.

ACTS 27 TO 28:1

He gave orders that those who could swim should jump overboard first and get to land; the rest were to follow, some on planks, some on parts of the ship. And thus it was that all came safely to land.''
Acts 27:43–44